*To my students and colleagues—past and present—
with gratitude*

PERSPECTIVES

ON SOCIAL
CASEWORK

HELEN
HARRIS
PERLMAN

TEMPLE UNIVERSITY PRESS
Philadelphia, 19122

Temple University Press, Philadelphia 19122
© *1971 by Temple University. All rights reserved*
Published 1971
First Templar Books *edition 1974*
Printed in the United States of America

International Standard Book Number (cloth): 0–87722–009–3
International Standard Book Number (paper): 0–87722–034–4
Library of Congress Catalog Number: 70–157736

Contents

Acknowledgment is gratefully made to the following publications for permission to reprint the articles herein:

Child Welfare
Minnesota Welfare
Public Welfare
Social Casework
Social Service Review
Social Welfare Forum
Social Work

A Guide
to the Reader
of This Book

Right off I must face my self-accusation: that the putting together of a group of one's own already published pieces and proposing to a publisher that he bind them up and put them forward, and nursing the hope that some readers will want to read them, whether for the first time or even again, is a series of presumptuous behaviors. Why, I ask myself severely, should these not just be allowed to lie quietly between the bindings of the journals that originally published them? This article may be scanned by the eyes, eager or bored as the case may be, of students, practitioners, and teachers of social work. That one may be touched only by the wriggle of the silverfish and spider beetles who devour all old journals, indiscriminately. Why gather them together and trot them forward yet another time except for reasons of narcissism, or reasons of fatuous maternalism, as one who says "These are my favorite children—I thought you might just like to take another look at them"?

So I hurry to explain—to myself and to you. There are some valid reasons. One is the fact that reprints of a number of these articles continue to be requested. So they must be thought to have some ongoing usefulness and liveliness. And there are no more reprints. But several other considerations are more important; indeed, they were the impelling reasons for my decision to make a book of these dozen articles. They are these:

I believe in casework. That sounds utterly naive, but I shall explain what I mean by that statement of faith farther on. Here I will say only that several of the articles chosen for inclusion in this book articulate my conviction and defense of the human values to be preserved and the human suffering to be lessened in a socially supported mode of help for individual human beings. Other caseworkers "believe in casework" too, even though we all know its shortcomings and the social conditions, whether within a single agency or the larger society, which may curtail its effectiveness. But in these days of rough winds blowing some anchorage of affirmation may be steadying to the buffeted ones among us.

Immediately a second reason for the choice and republication of these essays stands up to be counted. It is that threading through them one may see one caseworker's effort (paralleled and promoted by that of many others) to find, identify, and delineate the special "territorial imperative" of social casework. Over the two decades in which these essays were written the professions (and occupations) of "people helpers" have proliferated. Therapists and counselors by various names are ubiquitous, and caseworkers have sometimes had to scramble about trying to find their particular place and special function. At the same time, from within social work itself has come the upsetting experience of a kind of righteous rejection of casework as lacking legitimacy in a profession that must pour its resources, it is said, into societal, not individual, change. The trend in casework thinking and practice, maintained with some sturdiness despite (or because of?)

these pushes and pulls, has been toward coming to know its identity and its legitimate place in the family of social work methods. A number of these essays present aspects of that quest and finding of professional authenticity.

A third red-thread runs through a number of the pieces. It both dictated my choices and seems to me to be central to casework's present and ongoing concerns. It is the search for the linkages between the convictions that permeate and the actions that characterize casework and the living experience of the people with whom we deal. To put it another way, it is the probing scrutiny of some of the words and ideas that lie easily on our tongues in order to find what their actual blood-and-muscle meaning is when we translate them into action. So several of these essays are concerned with how and why people cope or founder as they do, and what practical implications for helping inhere in the understanding of their ego development and functioning.

Just as the development of the individual person in part recapitulates the development of the race and also closely resembles the development of all others of his species, so the development of a professional person both recapitulates and resembles that of the profession and his fellow professionals. This is the rationale for whatever personal references I make in what follows: it is my likeness to other caseworkers who occupied the same time and place with me, not my uniqueness, that is in point. I write of it personally because I was of it and in it, emotionally as well as intellectually.

The concern to establish social casework's particular practice area and expertise has been predominant in my professional thinking for a long time. It did not trouble me when I practiced and supervised practice in the two private family agencies that initiated me into social work and provided me over many years with a wide-ranging and rich experience. Their social concern for the well-being of families and individuals, their firm position as leadership agencies in their communities, not only as developers of the skills of analysis and treatment of individuals but also as effective spearheads for social change in the wider community gave their staff members a firm sense of who they were and what they were for. But uncertainties arose and proliferated as I moved to studentship in a psychiatric hospital where to my wide-eyed amazement, I found that not infrequently I knew considerably more about *their* field than many of the psychiatric residents knew; indeed, the head psychiatrist asked *me*, a student social worker, to teach *them*, student psychiatrists, how to interview for diagnostic and treatment purposes. Then, several years later, when I left the security of the social agency and went into a combination child-guidance/school-social work clinic I was further unsettled, this time by a very different set of circumstances. There was a blurring of function among members of the "team." Which of us undertook to "treat" a case, regardless of its nature, was often a matter of personal interest and space in one's caseload. In other instances I was aware that the psychiatrists were more involved and more competent in community social work (with groups of teachers, with meetings of school district superintendents, for instance) than we who were social workers. Was it, I wondered, their actual background of knowledge that gave them the capacity and authority to deal with "community"? Or was it their security in the social prestige of their profession that empowered them in their own and others' eyes? And what knowledge did a profession have to master and demonstrate to gain such security and prestige?

Part of the answer to that latter question was becoming increasingly clear. More and more social caseworkers seemed to be seeking alignment with psychiatry and its intrapsychic concentrations. Was this a matter of gaining status by association?—for there was no question but that the "psychiatric social worker" was at the top of social work's hierarchy. Or was it also (or mainly) our hungry search for keys to the many kinds of human behavior with which we had long dealt, knowing, humbly, that we understood it only in small part? Probably both of these motivating factors were present in the surge among social caseworkers to qualify as being psychiatrically sophisticated. But their expertise and identity as social workers was losing ground.

It was the recognition of these phenomena in the unfolding of social work that concerned me over a long time, both in my practice and in my teaching(10).* On the one hand my concern was to differentiate between social casework and other professional (or lay) forms of individualized help. On the other I sought to find social casework's valid place within the larger profession called social work.

Whether other forms of psychological influence are called "psychotherapy" or "counseling" or "client-centered therapy," or whatever, the plain-to-be-seen fact is that methodologically there is great similarity among them. This is not strange because all forms of psychological influence, the benign and the noxious both, are based upon the recognition and use of common human drives and common human gratifications. (Thus relationship with a helper who combines love and power, whether attributed or actual, is probably the most potent motivating factor in all forms of emotional-behavioral change.) This is why social casework both in its theory articulations and in its practices found itself continuously muddled over "the line" between casework and psychotherapy, between caseworker and psychiatrist or psychologist.

While our likeness to others, especially to respected others, had its assets and gratifications, it had its troubling

---

*Numbers in parentheses refer to publications listed in the Bibliography.

aspects too. The sense of autonomy and identity is as important to a profession as it is to an individual. It is not achieved simply by being "like" someone else, even indistinguishable at times, or only by swallowing and incorporating the strengths and skills of another. Parallel with the learning that occurs by incorporation and identification must come the learning through the exercise of one's own unique powers, within one's own life-space. The accrued experience of competence and effectiveness in tasks and relationships that have social recognition and cultural meaning (the student of Erikson and Robert White will recognize my sources here)—these, and only these, result in that secure and growing sense of "who and what I am—and what for" combined with the sense of self-respect that constitutes "identity."

The reason that delineated and felt identity is as important for a profession as for a person is that self-esteem of the individual practitioner is drawn in part from esteem of the group to which he belongs. Professional security, like personal security, is based on knowing the place and meaningfulness of one's home base. To know where one's roots dig in and know that that place has or merits positive social recognition is to be freed from excess attachment or dependence on others. It enables one to risk, to explore, to reach out, to challenge (without either fear or anger) the findings of others and of one's own too. It enables one to come together in cooperation with others, with no need to jockey for power or place, and no fear of being obliterated, for one knows one's difference and the values in it. The barrage of self-criticism within social work within the past decade or so has in part swirled around our failure to "innovate" and the dragging of our feet in the face of the need to examine and research our practices. Multiple reasons account for such truths as lie in these allegations. I have been inclined to think that our identity diffusion has heavily contributed to our alleged and actual timorous and conservative stance.

So I have tried to find the "specialness" of social work, particularly of social casework, its particular turf. If its methodology was more like than different from other forms of psychological influence, was its identity perhaps to be found in its content, in the substantive issues and characteristic problems that were central to its concerns?

Goaded by my own plea that we find the "social" in social casework(17), and supported by a kind of spontaneous renascence in social work of interest in social science, I became convinced that our special area of concern (and thus of our potential competence and expertise) was the enabling and enhancement of people's social functioning, both within that "system" called "person" and the concentric, enlarging circles of social systems with which he is in continuous transaction. I came to that conviction by small steps, through bit by bit explorations, explorations that continuously sought for the connections between my own careful observations of the stuff that people's waking hours are made of and my study of some of the newly relevant theory and research coming from the social sciences.

In 1953(18) I proposed that the "social" in casework involved our concern with "the person in interaction with some problematic aspect of his social reality" and "the client's ability to carry his social roles." To these I added the impact of social conditions and "significant others" upon the individual, the use of social resources to meet personal deficits, and the social nature and purpose of the social agency. In 1955(25) I attempted to delineate some areas of social casework's "as yet unsystematized and insufficiently conceptualized" special knowledge. In 1957(1) I suggested that "the person's being and becoming behavior is both shaped and judged by the expectations he and his culture have invested in the status and the major social roles he carries," and "the person who is a client comes to the caseworker at a time of maladjustment in one of his vital social roles." In 1959(30) I proposed that "social tasks" and "social relationships" were the substance of the caseworker's observation and helping process, and that the environment needed to be seen less as a "surround" and more as a living network of people with whom the client is in vital interaction.

By that peculiar twist of perception that makes even one's own statements when they are in print seem to hold inherent authority, these observations, strengthened by my study of the work of other social workers and behavioral scientists, set me off on a concentrated pursuit of the concept of social role in its relation both to personality development and to social casework's special domain. A number of exploratory essays came out of this effort(31, 32, 33, 34, 37, 40, 45). Only my first small thrusts toward finding our identity are included in this collection—"Putting the 'Social' Back in Social Casework" and "Social Components in Casework." Most of the explorations that followed culminated in my book, *Persona: Social Role and Personality*(3).

I record all this to show what a prolonged and often piecemeal process it may be to bring an idea to some fruition and to transmute it from hunch or theory to operational utility.

One may sigh over the fact that life is too short and that its arts, continuously stretched for, are only occasionally grasped. But there is nothing for it but to gird up again and sally forth yet another time. Thus, again, in the final essay included here, "Casework and 'The Diminished Man' " I reiterate my plea that in our careful attention to man's daily maneuvers and little victories we may yet find the powers and potentials for his greater satisfaction and stature. And that by such attention and aim we affirm man's worth.

To observe and study the ways by which people carry (or relinquish) their social tasks and relationships, how they cope successfully (or fail), how they make adaptations (or rigidify defenses) within themselves and between themselves and their psychosocial reality, is to observe and study ego operations and strategies. Hand in glove with social casework's search for the stable locus of its activity was its avid interest in and growing grasp of emergent theories of ego psychology. The concept of ego as consisting of those functions and powers that not only "mediate" in spheres of intra- and interpersonal conflict but that actually seek expansion and exercise in encounters with sources of stimulation is in full congruence with ideas about the vital import of social experience—role tasks and relationships—in the development of the personality. Inner and outer experiencing, input and feedback, is what "the ego" is engaged in from birth to death.

(Here, at the risk of getting lost within my own parentheses but in the hope that someone will one day pursue these questions, I set them down. In 1917 in a paper called "The Social Worker's Task," Mary Richmond said that skill ". . . in discovering the social relationships by which a given personality has been shaped" was part of casework's new aim; and in *Social Diagnosis* she wrote, "A man really is the company he keeps. . ." and "His social relations must continue to be the chief means of his recovery." What happened to this perspective in social casework? Was it perhaps that we had not yet got hold of psychodynamics and of how, then, interpenetrations between inner and outer experience occurred? Or was it that the psychology of the unconscious and the id in which psychiatry became immersed at about that same time focused social worker's eyes, too, upon intrapsychic phenomena with a loss of side- and outward vision? Yet another puzzler: In the first two decades of this century, four social psychologists, three of them at the University of Chicago, put forth some potentially powerful ideas for understanding the continuous interpenetrations between man and his society. One of them was John Dewey, whose thought influenced the group work sector of social work. Much later it was the source of my problem-solving model in casework. The others were George Mead, W. I. Thomas, and Charles Cooley. Briefly—and with consequent injustice to their ideas—they spoke and wrote of the emergence of selfhood from infancy onward through social transactions, of the "desires" that motivate action, of the "definition of the situation" as essential to the assessment of any person's behavior, of the personality as product of both "social demand and individual decision." Said Thomas, ". . . if men define situations as real, they are real in their consequences"; and that "social facts" must include subjective states and individual consciousness. The potency of these and other ideas of these now designated "symbolic interactionists" for social casework's understanding and action seem to me, who discovered them only recently, to be tremendous. Yet nowhere in the social work writings of their time have I found them noticed. Why was this, I wonder? Were they ahead of their time? Were their ideas confined to academia to which social work had not yet found entry and with which, therefore, it had limited communication? Were caseworkers engaged to the limits of their learning—for one cannot taste or digest everything at once—by those sociologists who were analyzing social problems and those psychologists measuring mental status? Did the empiricism and scientism of these latter groups seem more pertinent or "true" than the theorizing of deskchair academicians? And, since I am one who always seeks the lesson to be learned, is there a "moral" for us today in this tale? In any case, the work of these thinkers in relation to the development of selfhood through social experience awaits our scrutiny.)

A long, heuristic diversion, the above. To return to the pursuit of that knowledge concerned with people's use of their capacities in their efforts to function with adequacy and satisfaction: Any enabling of a person's carrying of the social tasks and relationships that encompass his social functioning must be based upon knowledge of what human beings need and want (their drives, innate and derivative), how they experience and read their reality (their perceptions and cognitions), how they feel about what they experience (their affects), how they act (their coping and/or protective behaviors), as well as upon the social actuality in which they operate. In short, any aid that aims to expand and strengthen ego capacities, developmentally or in the present moment's problem-solving must flow from some understanding of the ego and its processes. This is a second theme that threads its way through these articles.

Two circumstances combined for me, as they must have for many other caseworkers, to focus intently and wonder-ingly upon the forces for health and push and ingenuity that seemed stubbornly to persist in many human beings despite stress and adversity. One was the repeated evidence of these forces in cases one knew in both professional and personal life. The other, of course, was the unfolding theory and the opening vistas of ego psychology.

For several years before World War II, I had worked as both caseworker and supervisor of other caseworkers with a stream of refugees from middle Europe's fascism. It was a harrowing experience. Beyond the continuous fear and hatred one felt for totalitarianism and its bloody gut-thinking there was the daily encounter with men, women, and children who were its living, anguished victims. They were, to be sure, the lucky victims, the ones who had gotten away. But even they had left a trail of bleeding behind them, all the way from the place where they had been torn up by their roots from their homes and social connective tissue and had fled to this alien place, America, safe but full of present stress. Yet the persistence of the human drive for restitution, of the spirit that said "I hope," "maybe," "I will," "I must," "even so," was a continuous source of wonder and excitement to me. I realized that until then I had learned much more of the sickness in people than of their healthiness, and that I, along with my fellow social workers, had scarcely begun to scratch the surface of human potentials for recuperation and aspiration.

There followed on this experience a very different one. I moved in my professional work from this predominantly middle-class, suddenly dispossessed group to a lower-class, long-deprived group, from Washington Heights to the heart of Harlem, from one culture to a very different one, from white to black, literally and figuratively. Here I learned yet another lesson, one I had known before but which now proclaimed itself with the noise of thunder. It was that a long and repeated experience of being dead-poor, disadvantaged, stigmatized, closed off from the common good, a chronic experience of deficits of means, resources, opportunities or social recognition, will cut down the human spirit, constrict its capacities, dwarf or debilitate its drives. I became agonizingly aware of how details of everyday living may add up to a massive, overwhelming sense of defeat, frustration, and anger, and of how, then, to maintain social relationships and carry daily tasks, all the energies of the ego must be used chiefly to cover over, hold back, defend, protect. Yet, even in this squalid jungle there were, here and there, those persons, young or old, whose thrust and ability and determination to beat the devil—to study, to help the kids look forward to a better day, to hold on to a job and "make it"—leaped forth as affirmations of life and hope. "How do they do it?" was my constant question. "What feeds and quickens them? What inner powers do they have?"

Bit by bit the contributions of the theorists of the ego began to cast light upon long-neglected aspects of human behavior. Propositions about the autonomy of many ego functions, of the place of cognition and consciousness in

perception and behavior, of learned and culturally pat-
terned drives, of the innate push for what Robert White
has called "effectance" and self-realization, of the conditions, physical and social as well as psychological, that
determine motivations and goals; emergent studies of
coping in animals and children—all these and other
contributions of various psychologists began to expose and
explain phenomena that we had looked at but not seen,
heard but not listened to. And since much of what was
being examined was of ego functions in their engagement
with external realities, the nature of those realities (again,
the social conditions and situations with which the person
was in transaction) required fresh examination.

I have been more hungry student of than contributor to
the explorations. But in small part a number of my
writings have dealt with the impact and interchange
between the person's experience of some part of his reality
(casework help included) and his psychological reaction to
it. Within this collection several articles—"Are We Creating
Dependency?" and "Self-Determination: Reality or Illusion?" and "Can Casework Work?"—deal directly with the
import for ego development and functioning of certain
psychosocial conditions and their implications for casework. "The Basic Structure of the Casework Process"(19)
presents a tentative description of the parallelism between
the structured process of conscious ego-functioning and
that of the structured problem-solving process in casework.
It was the bud of the problem-solving model of casework (1, 59, 60). Among my other writings that deal in
whole or part with the psychological potency of social
experience are (8, 11, 15, 17, 18, 25, 30, 37, 38, and 54).
Of course the articles on social role and personality change
also contain these perspectives; they are integrated and
condensed in *Persona*(3).

There emerged for me now a new clarity and conviction
not only about the particular identity of social casework as

a helping process, its particular arena of expertise (actual and/or potential) but also its valid place within the total profession and practice of social work. If social work, in all of its various forms, is knowledgeable action to influence the nature and direction of both the social institutions and transactions by and through which people live; if the purpose of such influence is the simultaneous individualization and socialization of human beings toward their more satisfying and satisfactory coping, then casework is inextricably bound to social work. It is, simply, the method by which the smallest units—individual person and/or individual families—are helped to cope. If the enhancement of human "being" and "becoming" is indeed our field of endeavor and our profession of purpose, the substantive contents of our necessary knowledge and our potential professional expertise begin to make themselves manifest.

Yet recently, to the mixed bewilderment and indignation of many caseworkers, our authenticity and utility were suddenly challenged. Worse, the attack was chiefly from within our family of origin, with whom, at last, we were moving into full reconciliation. The critical rejection of casework by other sectors of social work has been two-pronged. One accusation has been that it is not effective, certainly not as a mode of social change and not even in its lesser role as change agent person-by-person. The other, less pointed, accusation has been that casework was not supportable in social work because, with limited time, money, and energies available, these assets needed to be poured into major societal changes that would make help to individuals all but unnecessary. Three articles included here were written in response to these accusations: "Casework Is Dead," "Can Casework Work?," and the last essay, "Casework and 'The Diminished Man.'"

Limited always by space requirements and my own capabilities, no article says all that could—or needs to—be said. The grains of truth in the accusations made against casework ought not be ignored; they deserve not fight or flight but our respectful analysis and weighing. I have tried, thus, not to be on the defensive about casework at the same time that I put forward what I believe to be a valid defense. I cannot conceive of a society so perfected that this man or that woman or this child at a given time might not find his normal coping and problem-solving in need of some outside support or facilitation. Nor, if I understand people's motivations at all, can I conceive of a social order where some individuals might not want more or better than they have and are. Yes, I can conceive of a society where social work is chiefly concerned with change in and management of social institutions, with prevention of social corruption and deprivation, with provision of enriched social opportunities for all people. (Then casework operations might be a minor part of social work—though I cannot resist the comment that it also might be considered a valuable "social opportunity.") However, how would we know the value and effectiveness of our social provisions and policies and programs? They would have to be judged, it seems to me, through the testimony of this individual man and that woman and their child who experience them. Even if only a small number of people in such a utopian society wished to give tongue to their malaise or distress under the Successful System, there ought to be the provision for their plaints to be heard and their greater gratification to be facilitated. That provision would be casework, by whatever other name it might be called. It would, I propose, be the only way in social work that the mass we call Society could be recognized as consisting of persons with faces, human beings whose very difference from one another is valued—more, delighted in. That is why I believe in casework. It is one of the all-too-few affirmations in our increasingly faceless society that you and I and he *count.*

As for the need for measurement and evaluation of casework's effectiveness: yes, and yes again. This must be our continuous, rigorous, and fearlessly engaged in effort because there are both mushy spots and atrophied spots in our practice and there are underdeveloped areas of knowledge on which our responsible judgment and actions depend. Only one "but": there will remain some things in any practice that involves encounter between two human beings that are not actually measurable, or even definable in words. I do not want to go misty-eyed over subjective experiences of "feeling better," "sensing wholeness," "experiencing difference," and so on. But to paraphrase Thomas, if men define experiences as real, their consequences are real, though they may not yield up the stuff for establishing proof. Certainly not until our research instruments are far more finely honed. Past this demurrer, I am glad for the many emergent efforts in the present day to try to test and thus identify what is valid, good, parsimonious, useful, in casework's methods and purposes.

*   *   *

Three articles I've chosen for inclusion remain to have their place here validated. I include "Freud's Contribution to Social Welfare" in some stubborn counterassertion against what seems to me to be an increasing tendency to wave aside Freud's thought as "irrelevant" to social work. My argument for his continuing recognition by social work, not alone by casework, is the burden of the essay. "Social Work Method: A Review of the Past Decade—1955-1965" is now a bit over five years old. Yet many of the problems and puzzles it records are still with us, still being struggled with, and so it seemed to me the article may still have timeliness and pertinence.

Finally (but first in line) there is "The Parable of the Workers of the Field," the oldest among these dozen works, perhaps the most frail; thus it needs justification.

From one perspective it is a period piece. Scarcely anyone whose first entry into social work has occurred within the past ten years knows what the diagnostic-functional controversy was all about. And anyone who did not live through it as a participant would scarcely believe the anguish and anger that tore casework apart during the almost two decades when, particularly in the circuit and environs of New York and Philadelphia, the "true believers" and the "heretics" engaged in battle. Freud and Rank were the respective philosophic fathers of these schools of thought, and I had often mischievously imagined with what utter puzzlement these two progenitors would have viewed their scarcely known offspring!

What some of us, licking our wounds, saw in this struggle was that for many of its participants it was more (or perhaps less?) than ideological. It revealed yet again the deep resistance to change that lies in all of us, especially when we are at a point of hard-achieved security: the distortions of perception and thinking that can occur when emotion rides high; the confusion between allegiance to personalities and allegiance to ideas; and the variations of defensive behavior that are called up when there is a threat to the established order—ranging from indignant self-righteousness to the shut-eye syndrome, the refusal to look or see.

From this latter perspective, this small fable may still have its moral. There are "sides" drawn up again today. This time they are not within casework itself but between casework and other sectors of the field of social work; and the issues are indeed of greater moment. But again one wonders whether separation and individuation and differences of opinion must inevitably be accompanied by such feelings on both sides as impair our perceptions and willingness to hear one another out. And whether there is not some way by which our common cause and the desirable diversities by which it may be carried forward can be steadfastly held in the center of our vision. This is why I include "The Parable . . . " here.

* * *

In sum: Here are one dozen essays from among five times that number, selected because they seem to me to offer perspectives from which to view social casework as it was, is, and might be. These are only one person's perspectives. But they have developed over a long and caring involvement in social work and in companionship with many other social workers. Perhaps they may serve as pocket-sized touchstones in what must be a continuous search by each of us for what is "real" and "important" and nurturing to the human spirit.

The Parable

of the

Workers of the Field

At this time in the Land of Us the sun shone gold and the rain fell silver and the earth was green as new paper dollars. But there came a day when a few people walked out of their gardens, and abroad upon the land, and saw that in some places the earth was sterile and stony and plants struggled to grow and were choked, and in some places the sun never shone and plants hung limp and gray, and in some places the rain never fell and plants shriveled and died. The people of Us sorrowed and said, "Let the soil be made fertile, let the fallow fields be planted, let each flower, each shrub, each tree, grow to its fulness so that the Land of Us will be as a garden." And certain men and women were named to be the Workers in the Fields.

In these ancient days the Field Workers were toilers. With their naked feet they trod the hot and barren fields. With naked hands they moved the stones, they broke the earth and sowed the seed, they carried water and pulled the weeds. Some among them had that grace of person, that nurturing touch, that later came to be called "green thumb," and under their care plants flourished and bore fruit. But all among them had the love of growing things and labored with the will that the earth be fair. This love

Social Service Review, March 1949.

1

and this will bound them together and drove them to seek out and to learn the secrets of the earth and of growth, of planting, and of nurture.

Now there arose among them a Teacher, a woman who was wise in the ways of growing things, and she said, "To love must be added art, and to art must be added means." And she gave to the Workers certain garments by which their nakedness was clothed and tools by which their bare hands were given new powers to dig and to hoe and to cultivate and to come to know more surely that with which they worked. Then wise men arose to give to the Workers a knowledge of sickness and health of soils and plants, of the strength and the weakness and the measurement of seeds; and to all these the Workers listened. They lived together in the house of their teachers and tended the broad fields in accordance with their learning.

On one day from a land across the sea there came a Giant, and he was a Physician of the Spirit of growing things. He was called Dr. Frond, for the great ferns of the dark forests that reach out their fingers to light. He knew how to plant and how to tend, but he knew more than these things. He knew the secrets of the inner life, of how the seed might be prepared, of the forces in seed and root that push to grow, of why one tree grows straight and one grows crooked. And as this Giant strode across the earth, the Workers gathered about him and became his disciples that they, too, might come to know the secrets of the inner life of growing things. They were at one in their humbleness and their zeal.

Now among the disciples of Dr. Frond was a younger Giant. He was called Dr. Rake, after a new tool that had been fashioned for gardening, to clear out debris and to make ready the soil for light and air. Now Dr. Rake was beloved by Dr. Frond, as son and pupil, and the wisdom and secrets of Dr. Frond were imparted to him. And as the younger Giant grew taller and wiser, he came to understand the use and the import of some things that the elder Giant had not seen. And they taught one another. But two Giants often cannot live in one house, and so it was that one night the younger Giant fled from his father's house and proclaimed himself his own master. And the elder Giant raged and mourned for his rebellious son.

Now among the Workers in the Fields there arose an echo of this mourning and raging, and anger grew among them, between those who best loved Dr. Frond and those who best loved Dr. Rake. Those who had been sisters denied one another, and brothers looked not into the other's eyes. For a time the delving of the earth and the sowing of the fields almost ceased, for the Workers turned to their hot fires to forge out swords and other armaments. Then the leaders among the Workers of the Fields built a stone wall across the land, and they said: "On one side shall the disciples of Dr. Rake labor, and on the other side shall labor the disciples of Dr. Frond." And each camp builded a shrine at which they worshiped their master and offered up appropriate sacrifice. But the younger Giant and the elder Giant did not concern themselves with this.

Now these were some of the differences between the Frondians and Rakians as found in the writings of those times:

The Frondians believed that the study of the laws of life and spirit in growing things was the first task. The Rakians believed that action to create growth came first. The Frondians said the Rakians were brash, and the Rakians said the Frondians were overweening.

The Frondians believed that in order to develop a plant to its full growth its fullest nature must be understood—the nature of its seed, its roots, its cells, the nature of the soil it grew in, and so forth. The Rakians said that if the plant were watched in one day's sun and rain and with one day's cultivation it could be known and made to flourish. The Frondians said the Rakians were callow, and the Rakians said the Frondians were confused.

The Frondians believed each species of plant should have such special soil, such peculiar gardening as was its need. The Rakians believed the gardens should be set for the best growth of all plants, even though one plant might perish therein. The Frondians said the Rakians were callous, and the Rakians said the Frondians were chaotic.

The Frondians believed that if a plant or tree could not hold itself up it should be bound to a stick and supported thereby till it gained strength. The Rakians believed that so long as a plant lives it has within it the means to stand on its own stem. The Frondians said the Rakians were unrealistic, and the Rakians said the same of the Frondians. And so on, unto the tenth generalization.

From the beginning it had been the custom of the Workers of the Fields to meet together once each year to exchange the knowledge and the crafts and the skills they had learned over the years, to speak together of their love of the earth and its fruits and of their duties toward it. After the building of the stone wall, one among the meetings together was set apart for talk of war between the Frondians and the Rakians. To this meeting certain chiefs came beating war drums, and the leaders danced before the arks wherein, broidered with purple and scarlet, lay the Books of the elder and of the younger Giant. It was whispered that scarcely anyone could understand the Book of the younger Giant, so deep was it; and it was said that very few had read the Book of the elder Giant, for wisdom is not read by him who dances. But this was held to be of no account, and the war cries and the smoke of ritual fires rose upon the air. Sometimes the leaders would speak to their cohorts thus: "Look upon this hollyhock grown in a Frondian garden," one would say. "It has been bound to a stick since it was a seedling, and it can no longer stand without a stick to hold it up." "Look upon this sapling grown in the Rakian orchard," one would cry from the other side of the stone wall. "A storm bent it crooked, and they have left it so, because they tend only straight strong trees." Sometimes from among the listeners would come a murmur that many other hollyhocks grew strong in the Frondian garden or that many young trees had been straightened in the Rakian orchard, but these murmurs were muffled with cries that these were miracles caused by unusual grace of sun and rain.

Nonetheless, when they returned from these conclaves, all the Workers bent to their labors mightily. On each side of the stone wall the fields and orchards and vineyards bore fruit. On each side small gardens appeared in the midst of deserts, and trees that had been dwarfed now flourished and spread their shade.

Now these were the ways in which the Frondians and the Rakians were alike:

They loved their work with all their hearts, and the fruit of their labor likewise.

They spared not muscle nor heart nor brain to gain greater wisdom and to learn greater skill so that they might make all growing things strong and beautiful.

They knew that the beginnings of their understanding of the structure of seeds, of the function of soils, and of the chiefest elements of nurture and growth were given them by Dr. Frond, the elder Giant, and that the beginnings of their understanding of their duties and their ways as Workers of the Fields were given them in the writings of the woman who was their first Teacher. And it is well known among men that the branches of a tree may grow to the north and to the south, to the east and to the west, but its roots are one.

And, moreover, they knew that all in their own work, in the carrying of their tasks, had learned new ways by which to do them. They had learned to prune the tree too thickly branched, to graft the fruit of one tree to another, to cut off and cultivate offshoots, to separate the wheat from the chaff. These things the Giants had not set down. The Workers themselves had created them.

And in the learning of these new ways it came to pass that the digging and the sowing, the spreading of soil and the carrying of water, the pruning and the reaping on one side of the stone wall and on the other were more different in the names they gave to these things than in the doing thereof. Moroever, it was known that the shrubs on each side of the wall had borne flowers that were of both sides and that trees on each side had borne fruit that tasted of the fruit of the other side. It was said that this was the work of ants that carried soil through the crevices of the wall and of bees that carried pollen over the face of the earth. But a few said that in the dark of nights certain Workers spoke to one another through the chinks in the wall and that what counsel they found good they took to their work in the Fields.

So it was that on the eighth day of a certain week a young Worker of the Field climbed upon the stone wall and sat her down upon it. It was a day of storm, of loud gusts of wind, and of blinding flashes of light. The Frondians murmured that the Rakians had created this storm by bad magic, and the Rakians accused the accusers. But the stripling who sat upon the wall cried out in a voice louder than the murmurings or the thunder. She spoke thus:

> "Let us have an end to the division of our house. Let us cease our worship of idols. Let us bend our wills and our strengths to knowing one another again. Let us cast out that which we have found of small avail. Let us make whole that which we have found good. Let us learn together of our differences, of the varied ways in which we labor. But let us speak together also of our oneness, of our kinship. Is not our purpose and our dream the same?"

Now, among the Workers of the Field who gathered near her there was whispering. One said that it was not known whether she was a Frondian or a Rakian. One said that it could plainly be seen that she was straddling a wall. One said that she was known to be the seventh daughter of the seventh daughter of the child who had declared that the Emperor wore no clothes. But there were a few among them, among the tall ones who could see over the wall, who spoke not but listened deeply.

Are We Creating Dependency?

Dependency is a bad word. It has done some loose living on the tongues of many people; it has kept questionable company with other bad words like "pauperization" and "welfare state"; it has been under attack by a group of highly respectable myths; and it has a way of making some people angry and other people uneasy. So it is most understandable that social workers feel some anxiety when they are accused of being instrumental in creating this bad thing.

The professional social worker has been trained to attempt to understand the exact nature of a problem before trying to deal with it. Therefore, I am impelled to take this bad word out into the light and see, first of all, what it is and what it means, and then I should like to separate it from some of the dubious company it keeps and from the myths that deplore it. Only then can we answer the question: Are we creating dependency? Then I should like to add to it another question: Can social workers do anything to prevent it?

Some Definitions

Dependency has been defined as "the state of being at the disposal of another, sustained by another, relying upon another's support or favor." To be dependent is to be unable to exist or sustain one's self or perform anything without the will power or aid of something or someone else.

Immediately we come face to face with a ubiquitous myth. This myth enters alternately slapping his chest and tugging at his boot straps. He announces in a loud voice that he is an independent man, self-made; nobody gives him anything, and he owes nothing to anyone. You will detect a hollow sound as he beats his chest, however, and if he hears but one voice of disbelief he will vanish into thin air. This is because there is no real independent man, unless he is a self-appointed hermit on a desert island. Every normal human being in our society is dependent in a number of areas of his living. We are dependent on other persons for their love, their esteem, their great or small kindnesses. We are dependent on the occupational functions of other people, on other persons' maintaining certain circumstances necessary for our well-being, on other persons' production and consumption. According to our age, capacities, personal resources, and life-circumstances, our dependency upon other persons and other things will vary in depth and scope. Total self-dependence is an illusion in today's interlaced society. The necessity to give and to take, to nurture and to feed upon, to carry certain responsibilities and to expect certain rights—these make up the normal balance between dependency and independence. This balance in the adult person can be called *relative* self-dependence.

Another confusion about this word "dependency" needs to be examined. In newspaper articles, in legislators' thinking, in political speeches, even in social workers' communications with one another, there has been a tendency to pair economic dependency with psychological dependency, that is, to speak as if the individual's need to take financial support automatically placed him in the position of needing to lean on others for support in other areas of living. Thus people who are economically dependent on public assistance are assumed to be less self-reliant, more lazy, less responsible, more weak, simply by virtue of their need for money that they do not earn. These assumptions need careful examination.

Economic dependency may be said to be a condition of having to rely upon some source of income that the individual does not earn by his labor or endeavors. Psychological dependency is a state of having to rely upon some human being's power, nurture, initiative outside one's self because of one's feeling of insecurity and helplessness. Obviously, all people, economically self-dependent though they may be, have moments or periods of psychological dependency, and some people who are economically self-dependent may be chronically dependent psychologically. It is also true that economic and psychological dependency may occur together. Either one may be found each without the other, and the existence of one does not automatically bespeak the existence of the other. Thus a man taking relief for reasons of physical disability may fully retain his capacities as a husband or father, a club member, a citizen—may operate, in short, like a self-dependent person except in the area of his ability to earn. On the other hand, a man with what we call, interestingly enough, an "independent income" may be bankrupt as far as productive use of himself is concerned, may be a useless parasite.

We are confronted by a second myth that beclouds our thinking when we speak of "relief" and "dependency" as if they were inevitably linked. This myth obviously comes from a long line of eminently respectable myths. You can tell this by the silver buckles on his shoes and the slightly frayed lace at his cuffs and by the way he looks down his thin, tight nose. Despite the fact that he is hopelessly superannuated and has good reason to be dead, he continues to haunt the premises of people's minds by asserting that only shiftless and immoral persons are poor—or, at least only these stay poor. Most of the people of this century in this country know that this is nonsense— yet so insidiously respectable is this myth that he is allowed living room in people's thinking, and they find themselves unwittingly believing in him and being victimized by him. We come out, somehow, tacitly accepting that virtue and vice are economic class attributes. As an example: depending on our particular sympathies, we flinch or we are indignant when a "chiseler" is found on the relief rolls. Is it not naive of us to expect that all the poor are or can be expected to be honest? Do we make such blanket expectations of people in other income brackets? Obviously not. Chiselers are found in economically self-dependent groups too—income tax chiselers, for example. And our reaction to those chiselers, too, is that they have been dishonest. But is it not interesting that no public voice says that men who make over $10,000 a year are all tax dodgers and that lack of moral stamina is an inevitable accompaniment to economic well-being? Yet generalizations equally ludicrous are made about all the people who are poor enough to need economic assistance. They are on relief; therefore, says the myth, whether they be young or old, Protestant or Catholic, male or female, sick or well, bright or dull, in chronic or temporary need, laborers or white-collar workers, all of them, says the myth, are alike—they are all people who are lacking in moral stamina.

The most troubling part of the influence of this myth is that the accusation of psychological dependency is leveled at the economically dependent as a way of degrading and shaming them, as a way of saying "they wouldn't be poor if they were any good." And because the economically dependent person is not a man apart, because he reads the newspaper and hears the accusations on tongues about him and perhaps even sees that accusation in the eyes of his social worker, he begins himself to believe it. He begins to feel like something less than a worthwhile person, like something of a second-class citizen, and self-respect begins to crumble. Psychological dependency may begin with such loss of self-respect.

As for the social worker, the necessity for his taking a good look at words and myths is not just a precious exercise in semantics. It is of considerable importance in answering just such a question as we face today. First, he must recognize that, despite all rumors to the contrary, the social worker does not create the situations that make for human need and he does not create economic dependency. Then, in order to answer whether he is creating psychological dependency, he must ask: How does psychological dependency come about? What is its relation, if any, to social work programs and practices?

Conditions for Self-Dependence

The push and thrust of the human body and spirit for self-dependence may be said to be born in us. It is present from birth in greater or lesser degree in every individual. Perhaps his comparative strength or weakness has something to do with inheritance or constitutional structure—nobody really knows. One baby sits like a placid Buddha and broods at the world and another dances out of its skin; but every healthy baby shows from its early days an impulse to do on its own in spite of the fact that its dependency needs are being met by loving, cradling parents. Every baby begins to kick and bounce, to grasp, to say, by its actions, "I do not simply sit and wait for you—I want, I will get, I will do for myself." He pulls himself up on the side of his crib, he crawls after a plaything, he mashes his hand into his oatmeal and pushes it into his face, he begins to venture about in the jungle of tables and chair legs, he experiments with the sound of crashing pots and pans, and often, when his parents try to put some limits on his exercise of self-dependence, he screams in protest at their effort to make him subject to their will.

Now, in the average family, along with the baby's own natural development, certain achievements are set up for his attainment, that is, certain expectations are held for him. He is expected to begin to use feeding utensils, to control his impulses to swat the cat or grab toys from a playmate. He begins to be trained to be both self-dependent and interdependent, to exercise his rights, and to take the concomitant responsibilities. These expectations of him will continue, although their forms will change. As he grows he will be expected to leave the protection of his mother and go off to school, to begin to study, to carry some tasks, to learn to use money, to plan in advance, to make decisions, to strive to achieve some place for himself as student or worker and, eventually, as key member of a new family. When he comes to maturity he will be, it is hoped, a person able and willing to carry his share of the load, able and willing to be a dependable member of an interdependent society.

But all this does not just happen. Certain conditions must be provided to make it happen. The basic conditions to growth in the baby, in the child, and in the adult are compounded of three ingredients: first, that feeling of safety, that knowledge of basic support that is called security; second, the presence of tangible material resources to use in play and work, and third, the knowledge that there is some reward for taking a risk, for trying—the reward of being loved or of being gratified. This is what gives the child and the adult free energy to reach out beyond himself for new learning and growth. The young child's security lies in knowing that home and family are a place where he is wanted and loved, that school is a place where people help him learn many things, that three meals and clean jeans and a pair of roller skates may be taken for granted; and when this security is had, the child is ready to reach out for new experiences. The adolescent's security lies in knowing that he is not a bad-looking fellow, that he is respected by his schoolmates and his teachers, that his parents, though they may argue with him, really stand behind him, that they will strive to provide him with opportunity to try his wings, and that his efforts to study or work will be fruitful. As we grow older we are secured not simply by what we have today, but we begin to have foresight and the need to have some feeling of security ahead of us. So the maturing adolescent needs to know that his efforts and his ambitions will yield him some rewards. When he has these securities he feels strong, and he is able to give himself over to developing his abilities and using his opportunities. In other words, in the average human being, growth, initiative, and self-dependence require a *floor of security* and hope from which to build.

Sources of Dependency

What, then, has happened to those persons who come to adulthood with feelings of insecurity, of inadequacy and fearfulness, who, whether they are economically dependent or not, are considered to be irresponsible or neurotic or dependent? What happened to their natural endowment of energy pushing out for self-realization and self-dependence? Probably something like this: Through the childhood and young adulthood of these persons the floor of security was missing—or, at least, was full of dangerous holes. Through their development they found evidence that theirs was a world to make one more fearful than confident. They experienced more hurt than comfort, they felt more deprivation than fulfilment. Deprivation and frustration can be of many sorts. They may take the form of consistently harsh parents who demand more of the child than they give him, who make more of his failures than of his successes, who, in short, fill him with the sense that "it's no use trying because I'm not much good." This kind of deprivation may occur in any social class, and among the rich as well as the poor one may find the individual whose life-energy is bound up alternately in despising himself and licking his wounds, and in hating those who hurt him. When we find this individual in the economically independent group, he is called a "neurotic" or is said to have an "inferiority complex." When we find him in the economically deprived group, we tend to say he is "shiftless," "pauperized," "dependent."

Another source of an individual's helplessness and irresponsibility may be those parents who unwittingly rob the growing child of his rights to self-dependence by carrying all responsibility for him, binding him hand and foot, as it were. Though their cords may be silken they are incapacitating to his self-dependence and initiative. The adult product of this form of deprivation will be found in all economic classes, too. When he is found among the rich he is seen, sometimes indulgently, sometimes censoriously, as a playboy or a mamma's boy or a parasite. When he is found on the relief rolls he may be a "good client," an obedient one, but he lacks "get up," and he may look to the caseworker to tell him what to do and how to do it; he is called "pauperized" and "dependent."

Yet a third group of factors may make for psychological dependence. These are experiences or circumstances an individual encounters that attack him so shockingly and overwhelmingly, are so deeply disappointing, that he retreats from the struggle with them and seeks safety. Safety may be found at some earlier level of adjustment where he felt less attacked, or it may be found in reliance upon something outside himself. In the economically secure individual the momentary cataclysm or the chronic derangement of his life-situation may be cushioned by money. It can buy him escape or substitute ways of seeking satisfactions, and his helplessness is mitigated somewhat. But for the person who has no cushioning, whose weakness is only emphasized by his being economically dependent, the sense of insecurity and hopelessness is likely to be heavy. Unless he experiences some relationship and/or some situation in which he can feel safe again, in which he can see a ray of hope and can risk taking another chance on himself, he is likely to resign himself to depending on what seems safe for survival, inadequate though it may be.

The signs by which one can detect psychological dependency are not that the individual gets aid to dependent children, old age assistance, or general assistance. They are, rather, the presence of feelings of resignation, helplessness, hostile pessimism, physical sickness for which doctors can find no organic base, passivity, and inability to mobilize the self to take necessary action or responsibilities.

Every practicing social worker can testify that the necessity to take financial help does not in itself create psychological dependency. The ADC [Aid to Dependent Children] worker knows large numbers of mothers. They keep their homes and their children clean, they cook the proper foods, they send their children to school, they comfort them when they are sick and take pleasure in them when they do well, they train them in acceptable habits and behavior—in short, they fulfil all the duties and carry all the responsibilities of normal motherhood. The worker with the blind knows large numbers of the sightless who maintain steady family and community relationships, who work at learning to occupy themselves constructively, who emphasize their capacities rather than their disabilities, who, in short, lead their own lives as responsibly as it is possible to do within their darkened world. The Old Age Assistance worker knows numerous men and women who

17

cook, sew, and care for themselves, who seek friendships and lend a frail but helping hand to neighbors, who, as statistics of the World War II period showed, literally rushed to remunerative work when it was open to them, who, in short, carry all the normal obligations of the aged in our society. The general assistance worker knows men and women who, despite the calamity that has resulted in their economic dependency, maintain good strong family life, go to church, vote, school their children, and hope and plan for the day when they or at least their children will be on their own feet again. (Incidentally, in a long and broad social work experience I have never known one person, not one, who looked forward to his child's growing up and getting "on relief.") All these people are psychologically self-dependent, responsible persons. They are sound citizens with empty purses.

Some persons receiving assistance are both economically and psychologically dependent. The proportion or number of these has not been established by anyone. It is a peculiar phenomenon that when one such person appears he is sometimes seen as if he were twins or quadruplets or, by that odd distortion of vision that bias creates, he is seen multiplied by the hundreds. However that may be, there are individuals—number unknown—on relief loads who are not self-responsible persons, who depend on others to do for them. Such persons are our concern, both as social workers and as citizens in a democracy. Our concern is that it should not be the social welfare program or the methods which caseworkers use that drain them of their self-sufficiency.

Every one of us knows that in order to be adequate to the day's work one must feel physically adequate. A headache can immobilize a person, a toothache can put all the feeling and thinking into one small cavity. When one is hungry, his mind is split between the task at hand and the demands of the stomach. In all of the common experiences of the human body we know how closely tied together are our feelings of physical well-being and our feeling of ability to cope with our small or big daily program.

Most of the men and women and children receiving public assistance today are chronically underfed or poorly fed. The so-called marginal food budget on which families on relief live is in the face of present food prices actually submarginal. As a woman who buys and plans family meals, I know the daily shock of seeing the chain store cash register leap to add up dollars for basic necessities of food, and there is no day when I do not wonder how mothers on ADC manage to feed their children well enough so that they have energy to play and work at school. Many of them cannot, of course, and they and the old and the handicapped, and those for whom no category of relief has yet been established, live day after day, month after month, poorly, monotonously, and underfed. Their physical energy is bound to be low. Their psychic energy is likewise sapped. The "get-up," the "go-after," the vitality, the planfulness—all those attributes that are the con-comitants of self-dependence—are, just like the budget, likely to be marginal rather than adequate. But, more than this, the marginal living standard has its constant psychic component. It presents continuous evidence that the world is a mean place to live in.

Under these circumstances what is likely to happen to the person? Is he likely to feel hopeful, optimistic? Is he likely to feel gratified and adequate to deal with his daily problems? It would be unusual if this happened. He is more likely to feel resentful or hostile, chronically unsatisfied—or to take on the characteristics attributed to him and feel ashamed and resigned and needful. These are characteristics of dependency. It is this experience of exhausting, pinching, and chronic economic deprivation of the barely adequate relief grant that can contribute heavily to feelings of psychological dependency.

At this point a pair of myths inevitably arise to confront us, and we must take cognizance of them. One of them wears his head backward on his shoulders. He is rapt in his admiration of the past. "In those days," he will tell you, "there were giants. In those days men dragged the stones that built their houses, they pushed or pulled their plows; women carried water and boiled soap and brewed medicine; children went barefooted and were glad to eat what they got. People would have died rather than ask for help—they were giants." This myth does not realize, of course, that only the giants had loud enough voices to tell their tales. The voices of those who sickened and warped and died before their time were quiet voices that could be heard only by those who cared to hear them. This myth's twin brother has eyes and ears stretched out of shape by focusing on far horizons. "In some countries," he will tell you, "people are satisfied with bread and cheese."

It is interesting that while both these myths are as thin as air they are not readily dispelled. What must be said to exorcise them is that "in those times" is not *now*, and "in that place," is not *here*. We are living, and so are persons on relief, here and now, in the second half of the twentieth century, in the United States of America. Materialistic values are high. One may decry this, but it is a fact. The things one must eat to be well, wear to be accepted, own to "belong," are infinitely multiplied over what they were even fifty years ago. Moreover, it is a time when knowledge of what people have a right to want is spread by unending communication from radios, newspapers, billboards, movies. Only recently the chairman of one of America's greatest corporations said, "There is a definite correlation between education and the consumption of commodities." Had he been speaking of persons on relief he might have added, "or in the sense of need for those commodities."

Every person's sense of his needs is greater, far greater, than was the sense of need of fifty years ago. My grandfather said that he never saw an orange until he was twelve years old, and when he ate it, rind and all, he wondered why people considered it such a delicacy. Nowadays every mother considers oranges a basic need for her baby's health. People's felt needs rise and multiply as standards of living rise and become more complex. It is fallacious to speak of days when one's grandfather raised seven fine sons in a one-room log cabin, because this took place in a different setting, a different time, a different culture from ours today. In a culture of one-room log cabins the seven sons grew up feeling equal to their peers. In a culture in which people are supposed to have bedrooms, the sense of inequality is keen when these cannot be had. In a community where bread and cheese are the normal diet, people will live on bread and cheese with equanimity, even though the sickness rate among them may be appalling. In a community where people know that balanced diets secure health and where, moreover, lavish varieties of foods spill over from grocery counters and colored advertisements, the person who must confine himself to bread and cheese feels both cheated and defeated.

The fact is that at our present stage of technological and psychological development nobody considers subsistence living to be enough to meet his needs. Sometimes we consider it to be enough for somebody else, but never for ourselves. Nor does the client on relief consider it to be enough for himself. He may feel it is all he deserves, or know it is all he can hope for. But, underneath seethes the feeling that there is a very great disparity between what he wants or thinks he needs and what his society gives him. He is left with a sense of being a second-class member of the community; feelings of frustration and helplessness may undermine the sense of adequacy and security which is basic to his self-dependence.

We said before that a potent factor in creating or abetting psychological dependency is that of hopelessness, of feeling that there is no way out, nothing better to look forward to. This robs people of all incentive. Yet, unwittingly, hopelessness seems almost written into some relief programs. When youngsters must leave school, not because they have fulfilled their capacities and educational interests, but because they are old enough to earn money to supplement the family's relief grant, when a man's or woman's effort to do some work brings only a threat of being cut off from relief before he has adequately tested the job or his capacity to carry it, when a man discharged from a tuberculosis sanitorium returns to the same skimpy diet and dingy rooms that first helped to inflame his lungs, when adolescents find that out of their newly won earnings they must turn over to the family everything but the cost of working, when a man found in the home of an ADC mother is viewed either as an undesirable source of income or of sin, when, in short, the hopes of bettering one's self, of having things different, are consistently cut off, then hope flies out the window and with it the spirit that makes people want to continue to struggle for self-realization and self-dependence.

Since a program of economic assistance is only a subsistence program, the individual will subsist, that is, he will exist marginally. His energies will be enough for survival and he will have little surplus. When a person lives at this marginal level for long periods of time with nothing to hope for, there will develop in him a sense of ill-being, of emptiness, of needfulness and hopelessness. These are the very essence of psychological dependency.

Therefore the adequacy or inadequacy of a welfare program—its mean or decent meeting of basic human needs—will have a potent influence in creating, abetting, or preventing psychological dependency.

The Role of the Social Worker

Now we must turn to the social workers themselves, those who administer and convey the assistance agency's service. Do they, by the way they feel and act and deal with people, create or encourage dependency? Or do they have means for the modification or prevention of dependency?

Social caseworkers may be tremendously important persons in the lives of the people they touch. This is because the client experiences the social agency largely through his individual social worker. For the average client, his worker's attitude represents the agency's attitude toward him and, back of that, the community's attitude toward him. As agency representative to the client, and as interpreter of client to the agency, the social worker is in a vital position to affect the lives of the people the agency helps.

By the way the social caseworker relates himself to and deals with him, his client's sense of personal worth may be enhanced. By the adequacy and dependability of the agency's helping service, the floor of security may be steadied. By the provisions of community resources outside the agency and the stimulus to the use of those resources, that sense of possible fulfillment, which is hope, may be buoyed.

In the run of everyday practice what does this involve? Everyone of us wants and needs the respect of other people—in a sense we live by the image of ourselves that we see reflected in the eyes of another. The more important that other person is to us—the more he represents established values—the more we want to be accepted by him. When he accepts us and shows his respect for us, we are strengthened in our convictions about our self-worth. That is true of our clients, too. The social caseworker represents the agency and the community, and because of this he is more than just himself to the client. The evidence he gives that he respects the client, that he is sincerely interested in him, that he appreciates his difficulties, that he assumes and affirms that the client has the full rights and responsibilities of a first-class citizen—this evidence strengthens the client's wish to operate as a first-class citizen.

Sometimes, either because of our own emotions or because of our lack of understanding, we tend to deal with the client as if we thought that economic and psychological dependency were the same thing. When this happens, we may be impatient, punishing, and over-authoritative or, conversely, overprotective, as if to imply "We consider you a bad child" or "You are a poor thing." The client senses this implication. He may react in various ways, but the end result is that he feels like a "bad child" or a "poor thing" and thereby his sense of self-worth is lessened. This has implications for what we do together with our client as well as how we act toward him. In the everyday interview with the everyday client some problems of his current living is discussed: How can I manage on my budget? How can I get my husband to meet his court order? What shall I do about my toothaches? What shall I do about my child's hating school? If we assume that he is psychologically dependent just because he is a client, if we assume that he is too dumb or too weak to think or do on his own, we may tend to think or do for him. The authoritative worker says, "Sign this, do that, go there, and for goodness' sake get going." The over-protective caseworker says, "I'll figure that out, I'll tell you what do do, I'll do it for you." In the first instance the client is robbed of his rights, in the second he is robbed of his responsibility; either robs him of the exercise of his self-dependence.

But the caseworker who understands the nature of self-dependence knows that it grows on help to use one's own powers. Therefore the caseworker offers help to his client in these ways: 1 He relates to him with compassion and understanding. 2 He stimulates him to think about ways and means of solving his problem, the possible action that he may take, the possible consequences of such action. 3 He makes known to the client the resources or means available to him. 4 He encourages him to consider what resources or means he may have in himself or his normal environment that can be used. 5 He helps him come to some decision on his own as to what is the best thing to do. 6 He supports him in taking the next step by the demonstration and the assurance of the agency's standing by to give him help in case he fails. By these means of engaging the client's active thought and muscle in working on the particular day's problem, we exercise his strengths and help him to know and use his own capacities. The dependent person begins to feel the pleasure of the emerging powers in himself; the self-dependent person has his strengths tried and confirmed.

To feel respected and to feel able to cope with the small problems of everyday living are basic human needs. To these must be added something that will enable a person to lift up his eyes from today and look ahead to tomorrow—some motivation to keep going. *Hope*—or the reaching out for something beyond today—must be founded on something real. To say that anyone can be anything he chooses to be, do anything he is ambitious to do, is simply not true. I assume that social workers need hardly to be told of the vast inequality of capacities with which individuals come into the world and the vast inequality of opportunity that they encounter here. This is one of the reasons for the existence of social work: that it should create or make attainable opportunities of which large numbers of people would otherwise be deprived. And this is why it is incumbent upon the social caseworker to do two things: first, to comb his community for those resources of medical, occupational, religious, recreational, educational opportunity and to help his clients know them and use them to enrich their lives; and, second, to make known to his own agency, to the churches, to the school, to men's and women's clubs, what resources need to be developed in order that the emptiness in people's lives may be filled. The blind man may not hope for sight again, or the aged for youth again, the disabled may not be well again, or the fatherless children have a normal home. But each of these may be helped to look beyond his immediate frustrations, may come to feel less helpless if the social caseworker can provide an injection of that hope that rises out of such commonplace opportunities as having a radio, going to a church social, getting materials for reading or handiwork, getting a set of teeth, garden seed, or a chance to go on a vacation. These opportunities empower people; they build up their morale, their feeling that life holds some interests and some satisfactions. Interest and some experience of satisfaction beyond keeping body and soul together—these are the bootstraps by which every one of us pulls himself up. Our clients need them too for the development of their self-dependence.

If social workers operate in these ways—by an understanding, respectful relationship to their clients, by helping them to recognize and exercise their own abilities to plan and work on their daily problems, by providing opportunities for the expanding use of themselves and for the hopefulness this excites—then social workers may be said to be ameliorating and even preventing dependency.

But the social worker too must be enabled. He must have the means and conditions of work that will permit him to consider and to do these things. When case loads are too high, for example, sustained contact with clients becomes impossible and only "hit-and-run" visits can be made. Under those circumstances there is little chance that the client will come to relate to his caseworker, or trust him, or find him a source of helpfulness. Nor can the caseworker himself, under such conditions, do anything more than meet minimum requirements of investigation of need and provision of means. Like the Red Queen he must "do all the running he can do to keep in the same place." When salaries are too low, the exhausting and demanding business of dealing with troubled people provides little economic reward or security for the caseworker himself. Then staff turnover and unattended caseloads will be inevitable. The too-high caseload and too-low salary are only two of the many administrative factors in today's public assistance agency that affect its workers' capacity to prevent or adequately to deal with psychological dependency when it is detected. Such factors ought not to be the concern of the social worker alone; they are the rightful concern of every citizen who fears the psychological effects of deprivation and hopelessness.

A critic of social work once proposed that social workers ought to stand, not for a "Welfare State," but for an "Incentive State." "Incentive" means rousing to action, encouraging, moving. To keep people active in their own behalf, to encourage them to move forward—these are the very tenets of social casework. From an understanding of the conditions that paralyze or motivate people, it would be hard to see how fear and want could generate incentive. If that were possible, our most enterprising and productive population would be the ill-fed, ill-housed, and ill-clothed. And, conversely, our economically secure population would be intellectual and moral sluggards.

Social workers know that incentive, like self-dependence, is compounded of many things. It is made up of wish for status in the eyes of one's fellow men; of the wish to occupy one's self with something that is rewarding and satisfying; of the wish for more of the good things of living than relief payments or insurance benefits will ever buy; and of the desire to be something better than what

27

one is today. We know, too, that in order for incentive, like self-dependence, to be sustained it must be underpinned by physical and mental well-being, by basic security, by open opportunity, and by some realistic grounds for looking forward with hope. It is those conditions that make for basic human welfare, for reasonable self-dependence, and for incentive that social workers must work for and help create.

Putting the "Social" Back in Social Casework

There has been a rather troubling trend in social casework in recent years. One hopes that it is symptomatic only of a temporary phase of our development—perhaps one of those excessive "swings" that may be found in the late adolescence of a maturing person and also of a maturing profession. It might be called an "intrapsychic-mindedness,"—a kind of concentration or obsession with problems of emotional or personality malfunctioning and with methods and schemes for casework treatment of these. That this is a proper and vital area of our concern no one would deny, but the trouble has been that another proper and vital area of concern has at least temporarily been neglected or cast aside as unimportant. This is the area of concern with what is maladjusted or sick in the interpersonal, person-to-group, social living of our clients and with enriched development of understanding and means by which the realities of the person's everyday living may be so modified or changed as to affect, benignly, his internal unhappiness.

The symptoms of this troubling trend are manifold and one need name only a few to have the problem recognized:

Child Welfare, July 1952.

There is some overdependence and clinging to psychiatry and psychiatrists for guidance, sometimes valid, often inappropriate in its negation of casework's own responsibility to identify, diagnose, and plan for dealing with the problem. There is, in some quarters, an overidentification with psychiatry, overidentification in the sense that there is some loss of the specific identify of social work; it becomes not an entity in its own right but an extension of another. There is some grandiosity present in our assumption that all that happens to a client, all that is vital and meaningful to him, occurs within the casework interview, and while it is true that this unit of experience can be deeply meaningful to a client, it is also true that he lives twenty-four hours a day, seven days a week with other persons and social situations that act upon him and he upon them. There is a concomitant tendency, with these other symptoms, to hold in minor esteem those forms and means of social casework that are not intimately associated with psychiatric auspices and psychotherapeutic methods.

The causes of this trend are multiple, as causation is likely to be. They lie in the very difficult nature of the problems that caseworkers encounter, so difficult, often, as to make us feel childishly helpless. They lie in our ignorance of the limits of what psychiatry actually knows, limits that the responsible psychiatrist will be the first to delineate, created by the mysteries—as yet unprobed—of how to help people and inherent in the special nature of the psychiatrists's job. They lie in our feelings of inferiority as we, members of a young and often unloved profession, work with a long-established and highly respected profession like medicine, and our wish to partake of its security and status by saying "me, too." They lie, too, in the fact that we have failed to identify, to express conceptually and to formulate for communication that accrual of knowledge of social life that has grown out of the daily work of every social caseworker and is the product of our repeated experience. There are certain areas of knowledge that are social casework's own. For example, the special considerations that arise out of the relation of agency setting and function to what can be done in treatment, or the possibilities and limitations inherent in foster home life for a child, but we have not put our accumulated experience into generalizations or principles that can be transferred from one social worker to another and used to illuminate one case after the other. For this reason, among others mentioned and left unmentioned here, we tend to lean heavily on a collaborating profession, psychiatry, which has consistently translated its experience into concepts. This, incidentally, is what Professor Tyler identifies as a distinguishing mark of a profession—"the basing of its techniques of operation upon principles rather than rule-of-thumb procedures or simple routine skills." [1]

This idea, that social casework suffers from a failure to express its social knowledge conceptually is not mine. It is propounded by Dr. Otto Pollak in his newly published book, *Social Science and Psychotherapy for Children,*[2] and I commend this book to social caseworkers because, it seems to me, it may serve to restore some balance in us between our respect for and valid use of psychiatric knowledge and our respect for and valid use of social knowledge. The theme of this book, as its title suggests, is that social science has much to offer in our psychotherapeutic efforts with children. The persons who were responsible for and participated in the inquiry and discussions that led to the writing of this book are members of a psychoanalytically oriented child guidance clinic staff. Their concern was to find (perhaps "rediscover" is the better word) "specific funds of knowledge in the social sciences which might be put to use in

1 Ralph W. Tyler, "Distinctive Attributes of Education for the Professions," *Social Work Journal,* April 1952.
2 New York: Russell Sage Foundation, 1952.

child guidance." Out of his two years' experience in this clinic, Dr. Pollak produces a number of useful concepts. One of them is that there are extrafamilial influences in pathogenesis; another is that interpersonal relationships in the family circle will be affected by change in one family member; a third is that there may be persons in a child's life as potent (or more so) as his biological parents; and there are a number of others. What experienced social caseworkers are likely to say as they read these is that they have known these things all along, and that is undoubtedly true. Yet it is also true that because we social caseworkers have not set down these "knowns," their *significance* and their implications for treatment have not consistently carried over into our operations. Our exploration of the child's social relationships and social activities and our engaging in treatment of those persons who vitally affect the child (not always or only the mother), or our efforts to ameliorate or to utilize constructively the child's vital social environment—these are therapeutic means that have grown remote and neglected as increasingly we have equated treatment of the child with certain controlled communications between him and his caseworker.

To Dr. Pollak's social science concepts, social caseworkers can if they will add many more that may serve to make social casework's contribution to the knowledge we seek in order to help troubled people. I suggest only one, as an example. It is this: The social problem of today creates the intrapsychic problem of tomorrow. There is no problem of emotional maladjustment in children or adults as we find them today that was not, yesterday, a problem the child encountered outside of himself—in the impact upon him of his mother or father or siblings, or playmates or teachers, or economic or health or housing conditions— in short, his intrapsychic problems have come about because on one day or over a series of days his social situation was more than he could deal with. This is a tremendously important concept for the social caseworker. Indeed it is the foundation idea on which social work is based, that the everyday life condition of the individual should be or must be made to be such as to ameliorate or, better still, prevent human misery.

Every day in his work the child welfare caseworker, like caseworkers in other kinds of social agencies, encounters unhappy, maladjusted children and grown-ups. They are not only the product of their past. They are being acted upon and are reacting to their immediate social situations. We need to know what these are, and what objective and subjective significance they hold for our clients, and what we must do to insure their being situations and experiences that are benign rather than devastating, supportive, rather than undermining of the individual's strengths. This means that along with our psychological understanding and use of that knowledge in helping our clients we need to understand the social elements that mold the individual in his daily life and to develop and use those elements, along with social resources and social services to meet his life needs. In brief, this means greater effort on our part to put the "social" back into social casework because it is basic to meeting the client's needs adequately. And, incidentally, because it will help to clarify and more firmly establish our professional identity.

Social Components

of

Casework Practice

"Social casework" is the name of our form of professional practice and "social caseworker" is our designating title. The best of our literature attests to our social origins, concerns, and practices.[1] Yet, periodically, we ask one another, "What is 'social' about social casework?" as if to reassure ourselves of our identity or to reaffirm our corporeal being. The reasons that push up this recurring question are severalfold. They include our absorbed interest in the inner world of the personality and some loss of perspective about the outer world in which that personality lives, our realistic difficulty in defining "social," and perhaps, as now, the need, in the face of pervasive threats to social welfare programs, to say again

The Social Welfare Forum, National Conference of Social Work 1953.

1 The writings of Charlotte Towle and Gordon Hamilton are rich in this testimony. See, for example, Charlotte Towle, *Common Human Needs* (New York: American Association of Social Workers, 1952), and such articles as "Client-centered Case work," *Social Service Review,* 24 (December 1950), pp. 451–58, and "Social Case Work in Modern Society," *Social Service Review* 20 (June 1946), pp. 165–79; and Gordon Hamilton's "Basic Assumptions and Methods of Social Casework" in *Theory and Practice of Social Casework*, 2d rev. ed. (New York: Columbia University Press, 1951), and "The Role of Social Casework in Social Policy," paper given at the National Conference of Social Work, Chicago, 1952.

who we are and what we know. I shall, however, limit myself to one task: an identification of those social components by which casework practice is characterized and vitally affected.

I shall take for granted: first, that we have never lost sight of our basic social philosophy, which affirms that individual human welfare is the purpose and the test of a society; second, that we know ourselves to be one part of the whole profession of social work, which is concerned with maintaining and promoting the social welfare of man in his society; and third, that we agree that the casework part of social work is a process by which certain kinds of social agencies give their help to individuals whose social welfare is threatened.

Perhaps the most obvious and yet most often overlooked identifying social characteristic of social casework is that it is practiced under the auspices of a social agency. Its methodology is based on such principles and involves the use of such skills as are common to many other forms of helping, counseling, and psychotherapy. But the distinguishing mark of social casework help is that it is authorized by that social institution known as the social agency or by the social service arm of some other human welfare agency. It is authorized because it is considered to be a most constructive way by which to give persons the help these agencies embody.

The social agency is an instrument fashioned to represent and carry out the will of a society. In some instances it stands for the majority expression of will; in others, for the will of some segment of that society; in either instance it is "social" by virtue of its goal, which is to maintain or to further the welfare of the individuals who make up the society. Every social agency comes into being in order to protect individuals or social groups, to prevent breakdown in the social functioning of individuals or groups, and/or to promote the development of higher or better levels of individual or group functioning. To these ends the social agency is maintained by the money and interest of large or small groups of society's members.

The social caseworker is hired to maintain and carry into action the social purposes of the agency that makes him part of it. The assumption, implicit or explicit on hiring him, is that he not only has know-how but that he is professionally committed to the attainment of constructive interrelationships between man and his society, and that he sees the agency as meeting, by its purpose and means, some portion of that task.

If the caseworker cannot identify with the social purpose that the agency expresses, he cannot, for all the skills and technical competence he may possess, act as its representative, and he should not in any conscience engage himself with it. If he is able to identify with the agency's social purposes but finds, as is not unusual, that it operates in ways that constrict or actually subvert those purposes, he must have some assurance or hope that appropriate means and channels may be used to make policies and procedures the servants of purpose. In any case, whether he is to be a reformer or finds himself instead in happy consonance with the major purpose and practices of his agency, the social caseworker must for the most part be at one with the social agency that he contracts to represent. This means that he is a carrier of the social concerns that the community has embodied in the agency. His concerns are twofold: that society and the partial function of it that is institutionalized in his agency be conducive by their nature and operation to the welfare of the individual; and, at the same time, that the individual be enabled to find and express his self-realization within the standards and values that society holds to be good.

All this has important implications for our practice and is most pertinent to the questions of our special identity and purposes. First, the social caseworker is not an independent therapist who has been given office space by an agency. Now, I have never heard anyone assert that he is. But, one often hears practice discussed in such terms as to lead one to believe that worker and client constitute a unit in themselves, housed by the agency, working with vaguely defined "needs" toward some remotely seen goal of "adjustment." The social caseworker can never properly take this anonymous role. The focus of his concern and work with the client is determined in large part by the function of his agency; the record he keeps of his work with the client is an agency record; if, for some reason, he himself cannot go on with his client, the agency is prepared to continue its service through another worker; many of the things the caseworker can or cannot do and some of the ways in which he can or cannot operate are determined by the agency's policies; and the goal toward which he and his client work, whether it be within ready or remote realization, is a goal that is considered to be, at the least, socially acceptable, at the best, socially desirable.

Now we face a second consideration that the "social" component of the social agency places before us. Since we have contracted to represent society's concern to help persons who are experiencing some maladaptation or obstacle in their social living, we are carriers of social values and social standards. In the light of this, our commonly held conceptions of the social caseworker's being "neutral" and "nonjudgmental," and of the client's "right to self determination," need careful thought. The fact is that as social caseworkers we are not neutral. We are for some things and we are against others. We constantly "judge," whether consciously or unconsciously, the actions, behavior, decisions, feelings, thoughts, of the person with whom we work. We judge, not in the sense of censoring or condemning him, but in the sense of estimating and concluding whether what he is and does is or is not socially acceptable or desirable. "Acceptable" or "desirable" by what standards? Obviously, the client and his behavior will be judged either by the worker's own personal standards and values or by the prevailing standards and values that society sets up the social agency to maintain or to further. In the first instance our client would be subject to the personal standards and prejudices of an individual worker, of which the worker may not even be conscious. In the second instance he and his behavior would be gauged consciously against that which society and its social agency hold to be conducive to the individual's and the group's welfare.[2]

There is a surge of discomfort among many social caseworkers as one says this. It rises from several sources: we have a burning conviction that the rights of the individual must vigilantly be guarded and that he must not be subject to any impositions of what he must do and how he must do it; and not infrequently we see our client victimized by the very society that holds him accountable and therefore we think we must come between to protect him against its depredations. But the reality is that we cannot pit a man against his society or lead him to isolation from it, because he is a societal creature. He knows himself only in his likeness to, and difference from, other members of his society, and his own conception of adjustment, like ours, is based on what is considered "normal" or held to be "good" by at least one of the social groupings of which he is a member.

This deserves far more elaboration than can be given here; for, as social scientists have made clear, social groupings within society are both varied and in constant

2 This has been well discussed by Grace L. Coyle in "New Insights Available to the Social Worker from the Social Sciences," *Social Service Review* 26 (September 1952), pp. 289—304; Sol W. Ginsburg, M.D., "The Impact of the Social Worker's Cultural Structure on Social Therapy," *Social Casework* 32 (October 1951), pp. 319—25.

flux and change.[3] Nevertheless, concerning the basic forms of human relationships and behavior there is a considerable unanimity of opinion as to what is normal and abnormal, good and bad, acceptable or unacceptable. That babies should be born within an established marriage; that children should go to school; that husbands and wives should live happily together; that parents should give their children certain conditions of nurture and care; that people should cooperate with another and respect one another's rights; that adults should carry certain responsibilities—these are but a few illustrations of the commonly accepted "oughts" and "shoulds" of individual behavior that our society attempts to institutionalize in its social welfare agencies. And it is as a representative of these that the worker meets his client. Let us be sure that the social caseworker will work with his client in such ways as to understand, relate to, and use differentially each client's individual motives, desires, and capacities. That is to say, the casework method by definition is an individualized method, and the goals, too, are individualized in terms of what each client wants and how far he is able to go. But both will be contained within the social purposes of the agency.

For example: The family agency represents society's wish to prevent family breakdown and promote sound family life. Immediately its caseworkers must be cognizant of what, in the large, is "good" and what is "bad" for family living. The mother of two children comes to such an agency because she and her husband do not get along. As she unburdens herself she speaks of her unhappiness,

---

3 See, for example, W. Allison Davis, "Child Rearing in the Class Structure of American Society," in *The Family in a Democratic Society* (New York: Columbia University Press, 1949), pp. 56–69; and various articles included in *Personality in Nature, Society, and Culture,* ed. Clyde Kluckholn and H. Murray (New York: Knopf, 1953).

her need for "self-expression," and confesses that she has been "experimenting with other men." As a person who is knowledgeable about human drives and behavior, the social caseworker will receive this woman sympathetically and understandingly. Personally, he may even find this woman's behavior quite acceptable, or he may follow the proverb *"tout comprendre, c'est tout pardonner,"* and see his help, therefore, as that of making this woman feel most comfortable within herself. As a professional social caseworker representing a family agency, he cannot properly condone or even tacitly encourage the way in which this woman is attempting to deal with her unhappy marriage. He is, it seems to me, charged with bringing the husband and children into her considerations, and with placing in the center of her and the agency's concern the fate of her family and its individual members. The way in which the caseworker will do this will rise not out of his feeling either that "she ought to be ashamed" or that "she has a right do do what she wants to do" but rather out of his twofold recognition: first, that he represents society's concern to promote sound family life if, in the particular instance, it can be achieved; and second, that the client herself says that part of her is strongly allied with that same concern, else she would not have come to the social agency with her problem. One further point lest this sound formidable: Society not only "demands"; it also "allows." It not only "requires"; it also "permits." Many persons who come to the social agency find in its realistic interpretation of society's standards the freedom to be and do what, before, they feared and could not allow themselves.

If the social caseworker as a representative of the social agency cannot be truly neutral, does the client truly have the right to self-determination? We know that all our rights are limited by certain responsibilities to the rights of others.[4] Within these limits, we struggle to realize ourselves and to assert what we want to do or be. Any valid and free choice of what we want to determine for ourselves rests upon our clear understanding of what the consequences of that choice are likely to be. The consequences we seek are those that will give us greater rather than lesser satisfaction. What will give us greater satisfactions in the long run are such actions as will not run afoul of what is acceptable by the people with whom and through whom we live. As social caseworkers we must recognize, therefore, that our working policy is not one of laissez faire; it is rather one of purposeful planning. We work to help our client make free and conscious and considered choices. We actually influence his choices because by our questions, by the considerations we place before him, by our examination together with him of his feelings and impulses and their relation, implicit or explicit, to social expectations, we attempt to affect his decision to act in ways that are compatible with society's standards and values. The client remains self-determining, free to choose the way he will go. His choice, however, may well be affected by the caseworker's holding him to careful considerations of his immediate drives and wishes in relation to social expectations and the adjustment he seeks, which is adjustment in his society.

Perhaps this pervasive influence of the "social" consideration has marked our major difference from other forms of helping or therapy. Certainly every social caseworker must stand for what his agency and his profession stand for—the welfare of the individual in its indivisibility from the welfare of the group. He stands for this, not self-righteously, or pontifically, or authoritatively, but in

---

4 For another angle of this discussion of self-determination see Helen Harris Perlman, "The Caseworker's Use of Collateral Information," in *The Social Welfare Forum,* National Conference of Social Work, 1951 (New York: Columbia University Press, 1951). pp. 190—205.

humble recognition that most human beings find and fulfill themselves as they find themselves in consonance with their society. Most human beings find themselves only as they relate to other selves, and they fulfill themselves as acceptance and recognition are given them by the significant "others" in their society.

A second grouping of social components consists of those that relate to the nature of the problems with which we deal—their social location, their social dynamics, and social means to their resolution.

The problems that a client brings to a social agency is perceived by him to be a problem in his social adjustment. It may be caused by a breakdown of normal sources of social sustenance, or it may be caused by the malfunctioning of the person himself; but in either case, the client sees and feels his problem in terms of social maladjustment because it makes itself known to him as he plays out his social roles and engages in his social tasks. Even when, as a disturbed personality, he is at the very heart of his problem he rarely comes to the social agency saying, "I, myself, need help." He says, rather, "I need help *in relation to* my unhappy marriage, my bad child, my mother's interferences, my schoolwork." He seeks a social agency because he assumes that it will relate to his social difficulties, to remove it or provide him with some way of coping with it. When other persons—laymen, teachers, doctors, psychiatrists—refer clients to social agencies they think of this source of help not because they perceive that the person is "sick" or "desperate" or "bad," but because they perceive him in a social situation to which those feelings and actions are related. And in the final appraisal as to whether or not the client has been helped, neither the client nor the worker nor the referral source ask whether all hazards to adjustment have been removed, or whether all emotional conflicts have been ironed out. The appraisal is rather in terms of whether the client's ability to carry his social roles and his normal life functions has been reasonably restored or bettered. This says, then, that as the client and the community view it, and indeed as the average social agency undertakes to deal with it, the person in interaction with some problematic aspect of his social reality is the focus of the social caseworker's concerns.

Within this center of our concern the casework practitioner has tended in recent years to be more understanding of the dynamics of the client's personality than of the dynamics of the social reality. While we have given recognition to the social realities of the client's past as molders of his feelings and character, we have not given equal recognition to the impact upon his personality of our client's experiences today. If we accept that the person has been molded by all his yesterdays, then it must follow that today's experience of satisfaction or frustration, of mastery or failure, will affect what he will become tomorrow. To put it another way, the meaningful experiences the client encounters in his social living today will be a part of his psychic experience tomorrow. It has long been a byword among us that our client's problem is always psychosocial. Sometimes I have thought we should turn that idea about and speak of our client's problems as "sociopsychic." The social components in all our lives are powerful factors in creating and affecting our emotions and attitudes, and we cannot truly understand our clients as persons except as we see them in their social context and have some sense of the significance of that context.

I think of the situation of a mother receiving help from Aid to Dependent Children who seemed troubled, but rather vaguely so, about the mischievous school behavior of her ten-year-old son. Her caseworker and the visiting teacher had several times discussed Billy with her, but her reaction was chiefly one of defense of the child and attempts to ward off knowing about the problem. "An irresponsible mother," said the school. "An inadequate mother," said the caseworker, more charitably. The social situation was this: The mother had been widowed seven months before and had just come home from giving birth to her fifth child. She lived, with her five little boys, in two rooms, on an ADC budget. The social caseworker knew these facts. But, like many of us, she was more prone to view the client from the inside out than from the outside in, inclined to place the problem in the mother's inadequacy of emotional response rather than upon the social situation that affected this mother's emotions and therefore her functioning. How could this mother respond vitally? Exhausted by childbirth, and perhaps by mourning her husband, she had to deal with the everyday business of feeding five mouths on a minimal budget, of worrying about torn pants and torn shoes, of washing endless diapers, overalls, and shirts, of keeping in order two small rooms that served at once for cooking, eating, sleeping, playing. How, indeed, could the woman find the energy to grapple with Billy's problem? Her defensive, shallow emotional reaction could only be truly understood as it was seen to be the result of a social situation which denied her, so to speak, the luxury of feeling. And it would be only as some of those social factors were removed or modified that the psychic and physical energy that self-mobilization calls for could be hers to use.

I dare say this is not an isolated instance. Within the caseloads of social agencies across the country are men, women, and especially children—those numberless children who are known only on a record's face sheet by name and age—whose social experiences are subtly but surely shaping their personalities. These experiences are not necessarily traumatic. They may never be recounted to a psychiatrist as dramatic episodes in the life history to furnish the key to the distortion or closure in some aspect of the personality's development. They consist, rather, these social factors that mold personality, of the humdrum

45

events with which the social caseworker is so familiar as sometimes to underestimate them. They consist of the relentless squeeze of poverty, of jobs that hold no present satisfactions or future hopes, of the want of meaningful connections with other persons, of days spent at school that seem useless, of homes that are only rooms and ugly rooms at that, of neighborhoods that breed the diseases of self-contempt and therefore contempt of others. All these social situations have emotional meaning. They thwart, depreciate, and corrode the human spirit, and the personalities that experience them will bear their marks. But, happily, the reverse is also true. As social stress is alleviated, as material needs are adequately met, as provisions are made for obtaining satisfactions that give the personality some lift and stretch, then the vicious circle of despair may give way to a benign circle of renewed energy and realistic hope. It is this response of the human personality to such changes in his social living as give him reason to hope, to aspire, and to have some present satisfactions that validates the existence of the social agency and the social caseworker. So skilled help in social casework must have as its basis a full understanding of the inseparable interaction of the living personality and its conditions of living.

There is much that caseworkers know about the social aspects of people's experiences that make them feel and act as they do. We need to name and formulate that knowledge more fully. We need to affirm it and utilize it as our special contribution in our collaborative work with other professions. But there is much yet to be known or to be lifted out from the individual instance and generalized about the social dynamics in the functioning of individuals. For example, we have long spoken of the family as an organic social unit, yet in our practice we have only begun to take account of the dynamic interplay between one family member and another, and of the shifting roles and operations that take place within this group. Again, we have tended to view our client in his problematic social role and have overlooked the fact that he, like all of us, may carry several other roles in his living from which he may derive strength or suffer devitalization. Again, we have been more intent and astute in uncovering people's "basic motivations" than in recognizing that the social behavior and the channels through which those motives are expressed are both the test and the means of adaptation. And so on. Before us lies a rapidly integrating field of social knowledge being developed by today's social scientists who, like social caseworkers, are organizing and bringing together their social and psychological knowledges. Already many of their writings offer much stimulus to the caseworker's thought and use.[5]

We have in our practice a time-honored way by which we have attempted to affect our clients' social situations but, for a number of reasons, it seems to have lost prestige with us. "Environmental manipulation" is its old-fashioned and perhaps rather repugnant name, but even though it has been renamed "social therapy" and "environmental modification"[6] it is often treated as something less significant or perhaps less requiring of skill than the one-to-one communication between a caseworker and his client. Because environmental modification is one of the distinctive forms of helping that social casework uses and is a form indigenous to social work it deserves some discussion here.

---

5 See, for example: Coyle, *op.cit.;* Kluckholn and Murray, *op.cit.;* Otto Pollak *et al., Social Services and Psychotherapy for Children* (New York: Russell Sage Foundation, 1952); David Reisman *et al., The Lonely Crowd* (New Haven: Yale University Press, 1950).

6 See Lucille Austin, "Trends in Differential Treatment in Social Casework," in *Principles and Techniques of Social Casework,* ed. Cora Kasius (New York: Family Service Association of America, 1950), pp. 324—38, and Florence Hollis, "The Techniques of Casework," *ibid.,* pp. 412—26; see also Hamilton, *Theory and Practice of Social Casework.*

To modify a client's social situation is in no sense a matter of "arranging" or "fixing" things. It is almost always a matter of influencing the feelings, attitudes, and behavior of people. It involves, therefore, all the caseworker's knowledge and skill. It is the activities, functions, and behavioral responses of people that, in the composite, form our social environment. Changes in this social environment consist of readjustment of living conditions, supplementation of inadequate resources, removal of persons from certain conditions of living, substitution of one for another kind of physical or psychological situation, and so on. Not only is the client, in whose interest the change is being made, involved but almost always there are involved those persons who are to be the instruments or the personalizations of the change. Placement of a child or of an aged person in an institution, the provision of recreational opportunities to an adolescent, the arrangements for a man's surgery, the readjustment of a child's school program, the staying of an eviction notice—each of these is an example of the caseworker's efforts to effect some "environmental modification" for his client. Each requires that the caseworker help the client to want to take his part in that change. Each requires, too, that the caseworker engage and favorably influence in the client's interests all those persons who will constitute the living part of the change. The child will know his new home through the new parental figures; the patient will respond to medical care in relation to the way the nurses and doctors act toward him; the child will fail or succeed in school in relation to the teacher's attitudes toward him; the adolescent will make use of the recreation group in relation to the group leader's understanding of his needs and peculiarities. It is the responses of these persons to the caseworker's attempt to influence their attitudes or actions that will result in the client's ability to use the new or changed situation.

All this says that the social caseworker, in order to modify the client's environment, must be engaged with the personalities that represent the environment. He will inform them, relate to their feelings and attitudes, discuss with them, interpret to them, advise them, support and accredit them—in brief, he will put to use all his understanding of people and their interrelationships and all the skills by which he tries to set change in motion. Perhaps as we take fuller cognizance of what environmental modification involves in terms of effecting person-to-person and person-to-group adjustments, and in terms of the import of these to the client's ability to achieve and sustain his social equilibrium, we will accord this means its rightful place as one of social casework's most valued components.

I have held my discussion rigorously to those social components in the daily practice of social casework. Partly this has been necessary because of the realistic limits of this paper, and partly, too, because it salves our social consciences too cheaply to give just a nod to the existence of those social problems that affect the lives of our clients but with which, on our daily jobs, we cannot directly cope. But one word must be said. There is evidence that there is receding concern with individual social welfare and a narrowing implementation of those programs by which people's social welfare is protected and promoted. Because the powers that affect social problems and programs often seem very big or very remote, we may tend to obliterate them from our minds and to insulate ourselves in individual interviews with our clients. And yet, no one should know better than social caseworkers the effect of economic stress, social censure, and restrictions or infringements of personal rights upon the physical, psychological, and social growth of people. We know something of the whole of social needs in the intimate living experience with them in our case-by-case practice. For this reason and for the reason that as social caseworkers we are social workers, we carry the obligation to speak out for the maintenance and promotion of people's social welfare. Our single voices are small, it is true, but we have something to say. Only as we say it, together with other social workers and other socially concerned persons and groups—for we are not alone in these concerns—will we be living up to the basic social component in social casework: the conviction that society must be for man if man is to be for his society.

I have tried to identify among the manifold components of the knowledge and processes of social casework those that characterize this form of help as "social." I suggest that the social philosophy that underlies casework, the social auspice that sponsors it, the social aims it preserves, and the social focus it maintains give it its special character. Our modes of functioning and our developing body of knowledge must take their substance and form from consideration of these components. It is not our methodology but the constructive, organized social purposes for which our methods are used that identify us both to ourselves and to others as caseworkers and as social workers too.

The Basic Structure

of the

Casework Process

In social casework, as in any other field of endeavor, the movement from trial and error or from stereotyped techniques to a systematic yet creative use of the self depends upon a lucid grasp of the purpose and organized form of the process to be carried out. It is an idea of this organized form and its purpose that this paper attempts to present.

Social casework is a process that certain social agencies use to help persons in solving such problems as obstruct their effective social adjustment. The philosophic commitments that this process seeks to bring into being, the goals that it seeks to achieve, the agencies that sponsor it, the skills that lubricate its movement, and the individualized forms that it may take are not here within our purview. My concern herein is only to identify the essential structure of the casework process itself.

As I see it, casework is in its basic nature a *problem-solving process*. The parts and structure of that process are essentially those of all effective problem-solving. I suggest that we examine this proposition in these ways: to state

Social Service Review, September 1953.

what the operations of problem-solving consist of and then to view those operations in the light of what people ordinarily do to resolve the problems in their daily living. The person who comes to the social agency as client is one who, for any one of a number of reasons, has found himself unable to solve his problem. We must look at the factors which underlie this inability, and, finally, we must ask and answer what the process of casework offers which helps a person move from some conflict or impasse in his life-situation to some more effective management or actual resolution of the problem that he faces. Perhaps it is only fair to warn you that you will not find here anything you do not know and have not already carried out in practice, at least in some part. What you will find is only some attempt to systematize ideas that are already yours.

All effective problem-solving whether in the realm of abstraction, within the four walls of social reality as in family life, or within the boundaries of the mind and heart of any one person, requires the exercise of certain orderly procedures.[1] They are these:

1. The *facts* constituting the problem must be known.
2. The facts must be understood, that is, they must be seen into in several ways: in their single significance; in relation to one another and their composite meaning; and in relation to the solution that is being sought. These constitute *ideas* about the facts.
3. Some conscious choice of action must be selected as *conclusion* and then tested for its validity by experimentation or reconsideration.

---

1 I owe the core of this formulation and the development of the idea of problem-solving to John Dewey's writings, especially to the chapter "Thinking and Meaning" in *John Dewey's Philosophy,* ed. Joseph Ratner (New York: Modern Library, 1939). After this paper had been written, I read an article which presents an interesting parallel to this formulation: George E. Gardner, M.D., "The Therapeutic Process from the Point of View of Psychoanalytic Theory," *American Journal of Orthopsychiatry* 22 (October 1952), pp. 669—78.

The analysis of these three steps we owe to logicians, but the operation of them for most of us has, through learning and repetition, become so habitual that we are scracely conscious that we take these steps. Yet even the simplest daily problem may involve these. "What shall I have for dinner?" the housewife ponders. Hers is a dilemma almost too trivial to be called by the ominous name "problem." Yet, how will this be decided? First, the facts must be examined, and these may include: what is in the refrigerator, what did we have last night, what does my family like, what can we afford. In relation to these facts, often simultaneous with them, will emerge ideas that will connect and endow them with meanings that begin to suggest solution. For example: It would be less expensive to use leftovers, yet my husband hates leftovers. Maybe I could disguise them in a casserole. On the other hand, if I skimp on dessert, maybe we can afford a steak. What this housewife is doing, even as you and I, is turning the facts over, viewing them in various perspectives, examining the pros and cons that they suggest, reviewing them in the light of objective necessities and subjective desires, weighing each of these in the effort to come to a conclusion. Sometime before dinnertime she must take this third step, to decide what she will do in the light of her considerations, and then do it. The decision will seem and feel right if no facts of significance obtrude in opposition to it—then the problem is solved in the acting-out. If, on the other hand, the decision is made by impulsive obliteration of the facts and ideas of one side of the conflict, the acting-out will produce a new problem. If you will take the long step from this mundane to a momentous example of problem—what, for instance, to do in some aspect of the international situation—you will find that the same structure of problem-solving must hold if action is not to yield even greater problems.

Happily for us all, we do not need to plow through each

separate step of problem-solving process for each of the problems with which we cope every day. Obviously, the more commonplace and more simple the problem, the more readily the mind leaps from fact to conclusion. But even with the more knotty problems we encounter we are not always conscious of our work at them. *This is because problem-solving may fairly be said to be the continuous adaptive function of the ego.*

The concept of the ego—with which we case workers are on such familiar terms and of which as yet we know so little—is, as I understand it, a concept of the organizing force within the personality. It is not, as our discussions sometimes imply, a strong or a weak second shelf in a three-tiered personality what-not. It is a concept that expresses certain functions of personality: the perception and developing of the conscious self; the differentiation of the self from other persons and objects; and the continuous operation of means by which to keep this differentiated self in balanced responsive adaptation to both the internal and external "others." This perpetually organizing force of the personality, then, works out modes of response and behavior that, while they maintain the balance of the personality, seem most realistically suited to overcome obstacles to satisfaction and to pursue personal goals that promise the satisfaction of the discharge of tension, temporary equilibrium, and readiness for new experience and learning. The so-called well-developed ego—which is to say the ego that is flexible, balanced, and coherent—is assumed to operate thus: It perceives: that is, through the senses, the nervous system, the mind, the ego takes in and records the *facts* of the person's inner and outer reality at any given moment. Simultaneously it responds in ways that attempt to test the meaning and import that can be ascribed to what has been perceived. Those testings are called "mechanisms of defense" or of "adaptation"; they are like the fine footwork of a boxer or of a dancer attempting to maintain both equilibrium and movement in relation to purpose. Whether the major pattern of these responses is withdrawal from what is perceived, or fighting it, or efforts to come to some workable solution, the defensive and adaptive responses express the ego's *"ideas,"* so to speak, of the meaning of the problem. The third aspect of the ego's function is to execute, that is, to select and act upon some mode of operation that seems or feels most satisfactory to cope with the problem that it has encountered. In other words, it *acts* out in relation to what it has perceived as reality and conceived as the meaning of the reality problem and its solution.

All these complicated mechanisms go on in all of us unnoted until we encounter some problem in the intellectual, emotional, or social sphere that suddenly makes us hear or feel that there is creaking and groaning of our hinges or that there is some breakdown or disorganization of our normally effortless problem-solving processes. At such times we set ourselves to trying to put some system or order into dealing effectively with the problem that besets us; and, if we are unable to do so, we often turn to another person for help. What is the nature of the problems that disorganize the ego's problem-solving capacity? It may be several-fold, and, whether we view it in ourselves or in our clients, it is the same.

1. The facts of the problem are perceived, and it may be, too, that its solution is seen. But the means or resources by which it can be met are not known or available to the person who encounters the problem. As we see this in our clients, their need for money, for medical care, for homemaker services, or for placement of child or adult may constitute for them a realistically insoluble problem for which outside help must be sought. Such problems, simple as they may appear to the onlooker, are rarely so for the person who experiences them because

they immediately affect the ego. The helplessness and frustration that we feel when our action is blocked by some situation or force outside ourselves may temporarily overwhelm or paralyze ego functioning.

2. The problem may be perceived, but what to do about it, how to tackle it, what choices there are and which are best—these ideas are confused or constricted. In other words, the facts are known; but their meanings, significance, and their relation to possible action are obscured. Sometimes as we see this in our clients or in ourselves, this is the result of misunderstandings or lack of necessary knowledge or information by which to think. At other times we encounter this difficulty in problem-solving in persons whom we think of as "immature"—that is, they have not learned to organize themselves to tackle the problem but have, rather, allowed chance, circumstance, other persons, and their impulsive responses to cope with problems for them. They have never systematically related cause and effect, thought and action, hindsight and planning, and when one day they encounter a situation that does not dissolve of itself or by-pass them they are trapped.

3. The problem or facts may be only partially or quite incorrectly perceived, and the processes of ideation and adaptation and action will likewise be faulty and inadequate. This may happen to any one of us, and we encounter it not infrequently in our clients. It may be due to some shocking event or threatening circumstance that arouses such deep and strong feelings as to overpower reason and defy conscious controls. Or sometimes the very nature of the problem may be that the person has become the victim of feelings that, disregarding the present reality situation, continue to govern and distort his thinking and action. In the first instance, an individual may be temporarily "torn apart," "frozen with fear," "blind with rage"—all these phrases bespeak damage to his normal

functioning. In the latter instance, the person may be suffering from an old disintegration that has been covered over rather than healed. In either instance, problem-solving by the person himself is made difficult and often impossible by these factors: The reality facts are not seen clearly because deep or high emotion tends to distort perception. The thought-processes that yield appraisal, conscious choice, reasoned behavior, which in brief facilitate adaptability, are weakened and tumbled about by the tyranny of emotions. The energy that is necessary to entertain a new idea or to experiment with a new mode of behavior is unavailable because it is being used in the service of controlling internal anarchy. The behavior, therefore, tends to be stereotyped and anachronistic, creating new problems by virtue of its inappropriateness.

You will readily see that no one of these kinds of difficulties people encounter in solving their daily life-problems is mutually exclusive. They may all be present at the same time in any one person. More than this, all of them are related at bottom in one way: they impair or they are created by some impairment of the person's ego functioning. His normal problem-solving processes may have failed, or are inadequate to the task, or, because of lack of means or opportunity, the solution lies outside the individual's power. Therefore the social caseworker's function, depending upon his appraisal of the nature of the difficulty, is to provide the means and ways by which the client's normal problem-solving operations may be restored, re-formed, or reinforced. I suppose this, in essence, is what is meant when we speak of "mobilizing the client's strengths" or "strengthening the client's ego."

As I approach trying to delineate how we may do this, I am aware of the difficulty one inevitably encounters when one tries to describe a whole experience. In actual experience one may know, feel, think, and act all at once; but, in analyzing experience, one must separate it into parts that, because one part follows the other in the telling, sound like sequences. What I am about to set down are parts of an interacting whole, separable only for purposes of examination.

Three dynamic means combine to make up the process by which we serve as aid and adjunct to the ego's problem-solving: (1) the use of the relationship; (2) the use of the social agency and its resources; and (3) the use of a conscious, structured problem-solving process.[2]

Basic knowledge about personality, society, social instrumentalities, and modes of helpful communication underlies each of these usages; they can only be mentioned here.

Of the use of relationship and the social agency, I can make only passing mention, too, because of the limits upon this paper and because both have been dealt with extensively and effectively in our literature and practice. This much should be said, however. There is ample evidence that in many different cultures, from ancient to modern times, and in all forms of the healing of the mind and spirit, the relationship between the helpers and the helped has been the primary dynamic of change. The conditions and nature of such relationships may vary, but at least two elements always seem to be present. One is that the helper is assumed to possess, or actually does possess, certain means or powers of knowledge, wisdom, or skill. These are what is being sought as the difference between the help-giver and the help-seeker. The other is that the helper gives some nurture—of love, communion, or gratification of some needs—to him who is to be helped. Both these elements are present in considerable measure in the casework relationship, controlled by the realistic limits of the social caseworker's professional role and purpose. It

2 See M. Robert Gomberg, "Counseling as a Service of the Family Agency," in *Family Casework and Counseling,* ed. Jessie Taft (Philadelphia: University of Pennsylvania Press, 1948), for a parallel formulation, to which I am indebted.

is this bond of nurture and sustaining strength that makes it possible for the timorous ego to venture forth from behind its defense works and to dare to experiment again with its healthy functioning.

In social casework the relationship between helper and the helped takes its purpose and form from the purpose and function of the social agency. It is the agency that contains, empowers, and gives substance to the casework relationship and to the business for which that relationship is formed. Its social values and standards, its governing policies and conditions, its enabling resources, give social casework help its special character of difference from other forms of helping. The person who has mobilized himself to seek the aid of a social agency in problem-solving seeks this form of aid in the assumption that the "know-how" or the tangible resources for solution are, in organized form, to be found there.

Linked to the social resource of the agency and sustained by the developing relationship, the third aspect of the helping process takes place. This is the reorganizing process of problem-solving.

In the initial phase of casework help, and at any point thereafter when some new or different facet of the problem emerges, the primary necessity is to be clear, client and worker alike, as to what the facts are. Sometimes it seems as though caseworkers tend to consider facts as dull matters to be got over as quickly as possible, so as to "get on with the case." What is a fact? According to Webster, it is "any event, mental or physical; an occurrence, quality, or relation, the reality of which is manifest in experience or may be inferred with certainty." The facts to be ascertained in the casework process are just such facts of occurrences, qualities, or relationships. They are facts of the nature of the problem as it is experienced by the client and as its actuality appears to the worker; the client's feeling and behavior responses in relation to his problem; his conscious efforts to cope with it; the available or achievable means by which it may be effected. They are the minutiae of "what is the trouble," "what brought this about," "so what did you do then," "what do you mean," "what would you hope could happen," and so on. They are the accounts of objective and subjective realities. They give "difficulty" or "trouble" their tangible and specific form, so that "help" and "solution" may be appropriate and valid. Whether, as the case might be, the problem is of insufficient money, of marital discord, or parent-child conflict, or of struggle against change, whether the data sought are of situation, event, action, or feelings, the guidance the worker gives by his focused inquiry is for the purpose of clarifying the nature of the problem to be solved in relation to the operations of the person who is struggling with it, in relation to the agency's means and modes for helping to resolve it.

The purpose of this aspect of problem-solving is so familiar to us as sometimes to be underestimated. It is the essential condition to the ego's primary function of perception. The ability to perceive clearly depends on a complex of factors, but that ability may be facilitated in fairly simple ways. All of us have experienced these ways. The projection of a feeling or situation in words, whether by speech or by writing, provides perspective. We hear ourselves and see ourselves with some greater measure of objectivity when that which has been in the mind is communicated to another. The separate identity of another person, with his differing perspective, offers correction to distortions in our view. As the other person, by his questions or comments, shares this differing perspective and as his attitudes demonstrate that he is with rather than against us, we begin to see through his eyes as well as through our own. So the client may find the caseworker's help to establish and clarify the facts of his situation an aid to his own perceptions.

The process that grows out of, and continuously interweaves with, inquiry as to the facts is the second aspect of all problem-solving. It is the phase of seeking to understand the meaning of that which is perceived. By analysis, imagination, reflection, and synthesis the normally functioning ego clarifies confusion, establishes connections, tests reality, and reorganizes experiences. This is the process of ascribing meaning to the perceived facts.

Several activities are involved herein, and they will vary in extent and emphasis with the nature of the problem. First of these is the separation from the melange of incident and emotion of some part of the problem as the center of concern. That part must be one that contains the problem's essential components as well as those of the client's typical ways of interacting with it. The facts of this partialized problem are now subjected to a kind of ongoing analysis between worker and client. The effort is to see its rational and irrational facets, its objective and subjective meanings, the appropriateness or inappropriateness of feeling and response with which these meanings are invested by the client; to gauge the usefulness or futility of his responses to the problem, to identify and weigh the pull of positive and negative feelings it holds for him.

You will recognize in this process a fairly common mode of casework operation, and its relation to the function of the ego is readily identifiable. A problem seen and felt as whole may be overpowering to the ego; because of its totality, the task of perception and adaptation seems overwhelming. When it is partialized, it is, so to speak, cut to size. The more troubled and disorganized the person feels, the smaller is the size of experience he is able to take hold of for consideration. The examination of the meaningful content of this concentrate of problem enables the client not only to perceive it more accurately but, by his emerging difference of idea of it, to begin to experience it differently.

A second way by which the problem is worked on for the ideas and meaning by which it may be understood and experienced differently is through the making of connections. This is the effort to put together what has been analyzed into more accurate relationships. Connections may be established between past and present or present and future, between act and consequence, or event and response, between self as victim and self as perpetrator. Our effort is to help the client account for phenomena which, as long as they defy his understanding, will defy his ability to cope with them.

In both this process and that of partialization the caseworker is active in clarifying, interpreting, supplementing by giving information, suggesting possible different ways by which to view what is under discussion, and so on. In short, the caseworker's effort is to exercise the ego in those mental processes that make intelligible what has been obscure. When meaning changes, our emotional response to what we perceive differently changes, and therefore our efforts at adaptation become more appropriate.

I am aware that, as it is set down here, all this sounds like a highly intellectualized process. If this were so, it would be of very little use to persons whose emotional immaturity or disturbance is at the base of the difficulty in problem-solving. Therefore I must hasten to remind you of these several conditions: These processes take place within the sustenance and feeling responses of a relationship. In any individual case their use is selective and timed by considerations of the client's capacity and will. Moreover, it is often the client's feelings and responsive behavior that are the focus of perception and consideration between him and the caseworker, not only his feeling about the problem he brings but about those problems he encounters in the very business of being helped. And, finally—and this we all know in ourselves—when, through the security of a meaningful relationship, we are helped to think about ourselves and our situations, that thinking together affects both the quantity and quality of our feeling.

A third aspect of the exploration of meaning is the discussion of the relation between what is perceived and now understood and felt differently to the solution of the problem. Here the active dialogue between caseworker and client focuses upon considering possible ways of acting, possible means by which to cope with the problem, weighing the pros and cons of decisions, rehearsing what might be said or done, anticipating outcomes, and making choices. This is the phase of coming to some tentative conclusion on the basis of having achieved a different orientation to the problem and a better integration of thought and feeling about it. Stemming from the choice or decision to action is the overt behavior of the client that will test the validity of the solution. Whether this decision to act in some different way comes about at the end of one or twenty interviews, whether it is determined or faltering, whether it consists of something as direct as taking hold and using some concrete service of the agency or as complex as a slight or radical change of behavior, it represents a mobilization of the ego to test by doing what it has learned. Or, to put it another way, that which has come to be perceived and experienced in some different way is organized for action in some different way and is tested by such action. If that action proves unsuccessful or unrewarding, this becomes a problem to be brought back into the safety and guidance of the casework interview for reconsideration of the facts of the inner and outer reality that frustrated the effort. If the new mode of coping with the problem yields some success, the attempted adaptation is experienced as satisfying, and the ego's sense of mastery and therefore of integration is at least temporarily restored or reinforced.

This, then, in the barest outline presents the idea that

the basic process of social casework is a problem-solving process and that its structure is essentially that of all effective problem-solving. All effective problem-solving involves ascertaining the facts of the problem, investing those facts with meaning so that they are experienced differently, and coming to some resolution that is tested in overt action or in the effect of changed perspectives and feelings. There is nothing suggested here that is not readily identified in casework practice. I have tried only to clarify the system or rationale that underlies our operations and to suggest a rather interesting parallel to the normal problem-solving processes of the ego. If this parallelism is valid, I think that casework help holds greater potential than we know for strengthening people's conscious powers of adaptation and learning. I think, too, that, as we take hold of the idea of an ordered structure in the casework process, we will find ourselves able to help our clients more economically, knowledgeably, and skillfully.

Freud's Contribution to Social Welfare

The influence of Freud upon every one of us is all-pervasive—all but impossible to measure or even to isolate for examination. So permeated have we become with the seedlings that were blown or drifted out from that small study in Vienna where a man sat and listened, and thought and wrote, that we can scarcely know in what ways we would have been different had Freud or some counterpart not lived. The ways we behave, our values, our thought associations, the things we say or desist from saying, the significances we impute to the speech and actions of others, our sense of what is funny and even of what is tragic—all these have been heavily influenced by this man Freud.

It is not important to the appraisal of Freud's contributions that many of the assumptions and guiding ideas we hold today were developed by the men and women who followed Freud or even by those who differed from him. He was their fountainhead. Nor is it important in assessing his influence to determine whether his discoveries were all "true" in any absolute sense—whether, for example, a death instinct actually does exist in us, or whether the

Social Service Review, June 1957.

Oedipal conflict is actually the core of modern neurosis. Columbus was not less a discoverer because he mistakenly thought that the island of Cuba was Cathay. He opened the way to the Americas and fired the zeal and imaginations of other men who were made able to venture forth by his rough, bold charts. So from Freud men had the first chartings of what the human personality was made up of. And in the same sense that Columbus was a discoverer of terrestrial space—that he found, explored, and charted parts of the earth of which European man had only some vague idea—so Freud may be said to be the discoverer of inner space. He too may have taken an island to be a continent, and he was surely not the first to recognize that, within the bounds of the human body, the mind and spirit hold volcanic continents and dark seas. But he was the first to dare to explore those unknown realms and to risk his professional reputation and his own peace of mind by setting down for the world to know what he understood and believed. By this he lighted up and reshaped man's conception of his inner world.

My task is to speak of Freud's contribution to social welfare in America. It is not hard to imagine with what astonishment Freud would have viewed this endeavor! Perhaps it is to placate my mental image of his questioning, incredulous face that I must stop first to clarify what this omnibus term "social welfare" means as I shall use it here.

Social welfare as idea and goal scarcely needs to be defined. Social welfare as work, social work, is concerned with providing such organized services and opportunities as will help people to cope with stresses that undermine their satisfactory social living and to promote their personally and socially constructive endeavors. It operates variously to reform, to restore, and to reinforce human powers and human institutions. Its processes are casework, group work, community organization, administration, and social research. Among these the one most firmly established by combination of its age, its body of knowledge and experience, and its widespread usage is casework. It is chiefly in relation to this social work helping process that I shall examine Freud's contribution.

And now my mental image of a listening Freud encourages me somewhat, even though Ernest Jones reminds me that Freud was a "revolutionary rather than a reformer." Yet, I remember that it was Freud who precisely pointed up the relationship between man's inner life and his externalized behavior and between man's experience of his environment and his inner balance. So I imagine that he will at least bend an ear to the idea that considerable connectedness exists between the theories he propounded and the development of American social work.

At the end of the nineteenth century, the American social worker and Freud were further apart than the ocean that separated them. At the end of that century of rationality, Freud sat in his quiet study in the Berggasse, surrounded by mementoes of man's ancient history, pondering on the irrational labyrinths of the human mind, its dynamics, and the deposits washed into it by waves of past and present experiences. What he learned of inner terrors and appetites confided to him by his patients, what he dug out and scrutinized in his own feelings, thoughts, and dreams, what he discerned from his wide reading in artistic, historic, and scientific literature—all these data and insights were the food for his rumination and analysis. Outside his quietly closed doors, the Viennese culture of which he was a part appeared to be a stable one, set and orderly, and even the keen eyes and sharp ears of Freud did not perceive the decay and running cracks that were already beginning to undermine it.

That same time in America was a rough-and-tumble era. Fortunes were being amassed, labor was being exploited, the industrial frontier was wide open, social mobility was rapid. Among those Americans who had the leisure to look about them and enough personal comfort to be able to listen to the still small voice of conscience (the superego had not yet been conceived of by Freud, so it was to conscience that the nineteenth-century philanthropist and social worker attended) there was growing concern about the disadvantaged people of the community.

Thrown together indiscriminately behind the ugly walls of almshouses were hundreds upon hundreds of feeble-minded and psychopathic adults, deserted or orphaned children, senile and physically broken aged, and wretched poor. In the large cities slums grew, sweatships multiplied, babies died of dirt and disease, small children were harnessed to long hours of exhausting labor, and the lives of the poor were a dreary succession of hand-to-mouth days. Yet it was a forward-looking, optimistic time when growth and change were everywhere to be seen and when it seemed to social workers that with good will, and faithful energy, and money, and the powers of reason, the evils that beset individuals or the larger community could be routed out. "The social problem with which the whole civilized world is now wrestling," cried a speaker at the National Conference of Charities and Correction in 1895, ". . . is how to reconcile economic and ethical law—the claims of business and of humanity, the decalogue and the multiplication table."

In this same year, Freud and his colleague Breuer published their *Studies in Hysteria,* and Freud presented his idea that neurotic anxiety has its origin in the sexual life, and, more important, his emerging ideas about the nature of the unconscious and the mechanism of repression. Had Freud appeared at the National Conference of Charities and Correction and presented his thesis, he would surely have been viewed as a madman, not only because of what would have seemed to be the patent absurdity of his ideas, but also because what he was saying seemed so irrelevant and remote from the concerns of social work.

Thus, Freud in the Vienna of 1895 observed and sought to allay some of the terrors and conflicts that ravaged the minds and spirits of human beings, and social workers in America observed and sought to allay the crude attacks of a raw social environment upon the economic and physical security of human beings. These social workers were already aware that prolonged deprivation warped not only the body but the mind and spirit of man and that the assaults of economic and physical stresses could dwarf or cripple man's personality functioning. So the "friendly visiting" of the poor and the distressed increased. Along with the limited money and medical aids that could be provided, the social worker of that day tried, by precept and example, by sweet reason and persuasion, by genuine sympathy and concern, to assuage the hurts and to lift the hopes of families in trouble. But there was a growing restiveness among these "friendly visitors," for the more they came to know people, the less understandable people seemed to be.

Moreover, they were increasingly encountering people whose behavior seemed to be the cause of their social dilemmas rather than the effect of them. There were those who could not do what they seemed to want to do and those who would not do what they could. There were those who resented advice, yet followed it, and those who reached out for it and cast it off. Here was an unwed mother who clung to her baby and here was a properly married woman who wanted to give hers away. Here was a woman who anguished over the sickliness of her children, but despite all her resolves could never get them to a clinic. And here was a man who brought his children strawberries when they needed bread, and another who beat his wife brutally when he was drunk and clung to her desperately when he was sober. Some of the social workers of this time accepted the then common explanations of these vagaries of human behavior—stupidity, ignorance, inherited perversity, and weakness of moral fiber. But others were not so readily satisfied and searched for deeper understanding of the human material they sought to influence.

At the National Conference of Charities and Correction in 1900, several ways better to understand and help the individual were pointed out by William Smallwood, secretary of the Associated Charities of Minneapolis. "It is the man rather than his condition which needs consideration," he said, in his effort to turn social workers' eyes from focusing on the social problem to focusing on the person who carried the problem. "To affect the life and character of an individual requires both self-discipline on the part of the visitor . . . and not a little knowledge of human nature . . . the man should be studied psychologically—birth, environment, education, life, mental and moral capacity." Then this foresighted man became again the child of his age, and as he sought ways by which to influence social work's clients he proposed that the social worker think, "Is there in him a latent moral force, a love of music, nature, sunsets and skies? Shall I have him in my home, suggest good books, good plays to see, music to hear and pictures to look upon? Shall I take him to walk with me into the country where the language of the birds, fields, hills and streams may be revealed?"

At that date, Freud was already undergoing his own painstaking and painful self-analysis. Ahead of his age, he had already written: "Certain inadequacies of our psychic functions . . . and certain performances which are apparently unintentional prove to be well motivated when subjected to psychoanalytic investigation, and are determined through the consciousness of unknown motives." [1] Only a few years later, he wrote, "It is quite remarkable

---

1 *Basic Writings of Sigmund Freud,* ed. A. A. Brill, M.D. (New York: Modern Library, 1938), p. 150.

that those writers who endeavor to explain the qualities and reactions of the adult individual have given so much more attention to the ancestral period than to the period of the individual's own existence—that is, they have attributed more influence to heredity than to childhood. . . . It might well be supposed that the influence of the latter period would be entitled to more consideration than heredity." [2] And within the first decade of this century Freud had already identified the major tools of psychoanalysis as "free association" and "the personal-emotional relation between doctor and patient."

It is doubtful whether any social worker of that era had heard of Freud or of his revolutionary propositions. Indeed, American psychiatry gave no hint of being aware of him. Yet the ideas contained within those two quotations and within Freud's discovery of therapeutic method became the nuclear ideas to influence all the behavioral sciences and arts, including social work. They were the core ideas in what was to become our highly developed understanding of the dynamics of unconscious motivation in the behavior of man, of the importance of the events of childhood in the development of man, and of some conditions governing influential communication between man and man.

In 1909 Freud was brought to America to deliver a series of lectures at Clark University. Freud, you may remember, once commented wryly that the only excuse for the discovery of America was the discovery of tobacco. It is possible that he would have found no excuse at all for the existence of American social work at that time. Among its leaders were women of a type Freud had scarcely encountered in his middle-European culture. They came of established families, cultured, conscienceful, yet unshackled, pioneering in spirit, dedicated to social reform. Their skirts trailed in the dust of slum streets; their

---

2 *Ibid.,* p. 580.

starched blouses were dirtied by sticky hands and heads of children whom they carried to clinics and settlement nurseries; their voices, gentle or strident, were heard in legislative lobbies, in courts, in local and national governmental bodies; their schemes and plans were laid before politicians, lawyers, clergymen, civic-minded men and women—and although they were sometimes looked upon with amused tolerance and sometimes with angry annoyance, they got things done. Together in co-operation with men of conscience and vision they gained the first pensions for widowed mothers so that children should not have to be torn from their homes just because of poverty; they promoted the establishment of the United States Children's Bureau for the study and promotion of all matters of child welfare; they helped establish the first juvenile court; they agitated for and won child-labor laws, better housing, workmen's compensation, minimum-wage laws.

Side by side with these protections and promotions of human rights went the day-by-day, less dramatic work with families and individuals—those who could not wait with their problems until a bill was passed or an institution established, those whose problems were the result of small, personal, corroding circumstances of everyday life, and those who, out of some dark inner life, seemed to create their own problems.

As social workers bent to these daily tasks—coaxing this mother to send her children to the settlement, exhorting that father to give up alcohol, finding money for a pair of blue serge pants in which a boy could graduate, teaching a family how to manage within its skimpy means—they searched for better understanding of the people whom they were trying to influence. They could not fully explain either their successes or their failures. Increasingly they looked to the developing fields of psychology and psychiatry for guidance.

Montaigne once said, "The arts and sciences are not cast

from a mold; they are shaped and polished little by little, here a dab and there a pat—as bears leisurely lick their cubs into shape." The arts and science of social work, too, grew this way. Freud's contributions came not as sudden revelation, but rather as a dab here and a pat there, a trickle of insight in one place, a widening of understanding in another, hastening, but almost imperceptibly, the evolution and development of social work's knowledge and methods.

At first, the ideas of Freud filtered through to social work not directly from his writings but indirectly through the few psychologists and psychiatrists who in clinics and hospitals worked in frequent collaboration with social workers in the stubborn problems of personality distortion and breakdown. These men found in Freud's writings (there were scarcely more than a dozen publications on or about Freudian thought in America by 1917) both support and stimulus to their own emerging ideas and observations. By that well-known phenomenon of the spontaneous production of like ideas in different minds at the same time, a number of American psychiatrists and psychologists had begun experimentally to test ideas coming from Germany, Switzerland, and Vienna and to connect them with hypotheses and methods of their own. Freud's ideas were particularly notable and potent, not only because of their original and seminal nature, but because, when they aroused violent opposition, they forced the antagonist to formulate his countertheories more precisely, and because so often they flung back the mind's shutters and poured a flood of light upon truths already lurking there but only half-perceived.

It is no wonder that social workers grasped eagerly at Freudian ideas when they began to filter through. Social workers had long observed and pondered on the "psychopathology of everyday life" (if I may use Freud's phrase in this different sense). They had long worked to sustain

73

good family life, and to provide physical, emotional, and educational opportunities for children. Much of what Freud had to say about childhood found responsive echoes in social workers' experiences. Moreover, as World War I brought many middle-class families to social agencies and as young men of "good" background broke down under battle stress, it became clear that certain circumstances can rock the emotional balance of the best of us, and that the then-current theories of mental and social deficiency left much to be explained. So it was that by the end of the second decade after Freud had made his major discoveries, social caseworkers keenly felt the need of them and had become psychologically oriented enough to be able to entertain them. They set about translating them from the language and practices of psychoanalysis into language and practices of social casework.

I have stated that Freud's major contributions to social work—and perhaps to all humanistic endeavors—were three-fold: his discoveries of the powers of the un-conscious mind, his discovery of the importance of childhood experiences, and his discovery of certain vital therapeutic means. It behooves me now to translate these into their usefulness for social work.

Poets, philosophers, physicians, and even the ordinary man guessed or knew of the existence of the unconscious mind long before Freud. It was Freud, however, who was bold enough to dare to identify its contents and powers. The method by which he developed and tested his hypotheses was in itself a stroke of genius. There is no room to discuss here his analysis of dreams, of hypnotic behavior, of slips of the tongue, of uninhibited speech productions—all of man's unwilled communications. What his searches made apparent was that man's unconscious mind is a powerhouse of drives pushing to take in or to find expression in satisfying experience and, at other times, pushing to avoid or blot out what is experienced as frustrating or dangerous. From out of this chaotic but purposive inner universe the conscious mind develops as a new world of order and control, but it is subject to interference and government by unconscious forces. The purpose behind all and any behavior, even unreasonable behavior, is man's need to satisfy his hungers—whether for food, love, status—and to discharge his energies in ways that yield him a sense of pleasure rather than frustration. But some hungers of the unconscious may not be acceptable to the conscious mind, Freud saw, and must be denied or diverted or held under. And often, Freud pointed out, the person's emotion-charged wants or needs are unrecognized by their possessor and make him act and feel in ways that his consciousness finds alien and yet uncontrollable. Sometimes the heart and the head of man are in continuous warfare, and at other times the head cloaks the heart's reasons in the becoming garments of rationality and thus admits them to consciousness. In short, Freud revealed to us the meaning of behavior, whether overt or inner, and the forces and balances which propel it.

It is a disconcerting, even distressing moment, that moment when one realizes that one is not fully master of his soul. But it may be a humanizing moment, too, because it is then that he knows himself to be one with all other human beings. This is to know that his virtues as well as his vices, his successes as well as his failures, are heavily predetermined by the play of unconscious forces that, at base, are the same as those in every other man.

These insights affected social workers deeply. Moralistic self-righteousness cannot be sustained under their searching light. As a result, social workers came to feel more humble, more self-aware, and thus more self-disciplined and more deeply compassionate in the presence of human fraility and pain.

The changes in our practice that followed on these

insights are so many and so complex as to allow only their identification, not their description, here. As we came to understand more deeply the purposiveness of behavior and the role of unconscious force, the doors to many mysteries of human behavior opened to us. Now we could understand that a woman's sexual promiscuity could rise, not out of uncontrolled lust, but out of a need to feel loved, if only briefly and crudely; that a mother's neglect of her child occurred, not because she did not know what child care involved, but because she herself still needed and sought mothering; that a man who on every job quarreled with his boss was still fighting the image of his harsh, authoritative father. In short, we came to see the psychodynamics beneath the surface symptom.

The value in this was not that by understanding all we could forgive all. Rather it was that we could begin to grapple with some of the problems of cause rather than those of effect. To do this, we came to know that we had to relate ourselves to our troubled client in consideration of what it was he wanted, what his hunger and aim were. Thus, his motivation rather than ours became the propelling force, and he could become an actor in his own problem-solving task rather than, as before, a recipient of such guidance as an active caseworker could give. Toward this end, we learned to enable our client to express and examine his own feelings and attitudes that, formerly, as we had appealed to his conscious reason, had been cloaked or glossed over. Now he came to know and to be better able to cope with some of the unreasonable forces that held him in their grip. As our knowledge and skills grew, the whole practice of social casework expanded to include work with the many problems of psychological as well as social stress as they arose in people's daily functioning.

As soon as one becomes a close observer of human behavior and notes the differing ways people react to like circumstances, one asks: "How is this? How is it that one man responds to adversity by mobilizing all his energies, while another collapses? That one family on relief maintains all its self-reliance and another sinks into apathy? That one child in a family becomes a delinquent and another shines among his peers?"

It was by his answers to these questions that Freud made his second great contribution. This was his discovery of the vital importance of the experiences of childhood in the formation of the character and personality. To be sure, we had long known that "as the twig is bent so grows the tree" and that "the child is father to the man." Yet well into the present century the child was generally conceived of as an adult in miniature, and his personality was assumed to have been set by inheritance or by special grace of God or interferences of the devil, all subject, to be sure, to responsible parental guidance. What Freud learned from his patients as they poured out their childhood memories and their still childish desires and fears was the dynamic significance of the everyday taken-for-granted occurrences in the life of the child. All the small ways by which babies and young children come to feel and to perceive their world and themselves in relation to it—all the little experiences of physical and emotional warmth or coldness, tenderness or harshness, all the communications from the arms and eyes and lips of parents—all these bits of the growth of the inner child were suddenly opened to view by Freud's theories. What Freud said about the child's life was met at first with shocked incredulity or derision for he wrote of the "sexual" needs and gratifications of babies and children. But those who paused to listen to him and to look at children through newly inquiring eyes came to understand that by "sexual" Freud meant not only the frank interest that every child comes to have in his own body and in the bodies of other people but—and chiefly this—all the "tender-affectionate-sensual" experiences that every child needs in order to feel loved and loving.

The idea that good family life is the cradle of the child's emotional as well as physical well-being has been a basic tenet in social work. Over one hundred years ago, Charles Loring Brace, pioneer child welfare worker, launched the foster-home movement so that abandoned, neglected and troublesome children could become members of families. "Children are more likely to turn out well in a family than in a reformatory," he wrote at a time when this was a radical idea. Perhaps the most powerful motivation in American social work has been concern that childhood should be a time of nurture and sturdy growth. Yet, until Freud opened up the inner world of childhood, the conception of the child's needs was a fairly simple one—the provision of food and shelter, cleanliness, and parental guidance.

Freud set down clearly that neurosis is the product of a child's interaction with his social environment ("social restrictions," Freud called them, in his repressive nineteenth-century climate), and, as social workers lent themselves to understanding what his meaning was, they saw with sudden clarity what they had long observed and experienced in their work with families and children. By all the small events of being fed or left hungry, of being helped or hurt, of knowing a mother and father as good and reliable or as bad and undependable, of seeing acceptance in the eyes of a teacher or finding indifference there, of feeling that the small world of "home" is a place of warmth and shelter, psychologically as well as physically, or that it is frustrating and empty—by all these experiences of his everyday life is the child's inner security, his self-esteem, his forward striving built or destroyed. By these he is readied for adulthood.

So, today's child welfare worker strives, not only for the physical well-being of the child, but for his emotional well-being too. The family welfare worker is concerned, not only to keep the family together under one roof and at one table, but also to help husband and wife to attain the mutual tolerance, at least, or tender affection, at best, that enables them to lend themselves to their children's needs. The public assistance worker has come to grasp the emotional import to children and their parents of economic pinching and restrictions, and to see how initiative and self-esteem may die and how apathy and resignation flourish if life seems stagnant and hopeless. The school social worker has come to interpret to teachers and parents the relatedness of a child's learning problems or behavior difficulties to his family situation and to the sustainment and satisfaction that school may provide or deny him. The child-guidance caseworker, employed with problems of children already troubled within themselves or in relation to others, seeks carefully to find and then to modify those actions and circumstances in the child's life that rouse his fears and threaten his sense of balance.

All these efforts by social workers to influence benignly the growth and social functioning of the human personality are dependent upon the ability to communicate with people, i.e., upon the ability to hear what a person says, to know exactly what he means by what he says, and then to respond to him in such ways that he in turn can take in what is meant. It is to this development of the science and art of therapeutic communication that Freud made his third signal contribution.

The art of influencing human behavior through verbal suggestion and persuasion is as old as man, and communication to man's unconscious was the stock-in-trade of seers, oracles, witch doctors, and saints. When Freud in his early days spoke to the unconscious minds of his disturbed patients through hypnosis, he was engaged in an ancient practice. But he abandoned it shortly, for a reason that seems obvious to us now but was revolutionary when he formulated it. Within hypnosis or other potent forms of suggestion, Freud saw that the patient's unconscious was brought into communication with the conscious ideas and will of another and that when the influence of that "other" wore off the patient was again prey to his internal disorders. Thus, Freud saw that if a man was to become master rather than victim of his unconscious desires and fears he would need to have his own internal communication system established and in working order. The patient's conscious, rational mind must come to know and speak with his unconscious and thus gain greater possession and control of its power. To this end Freud hit on the method of "free association"—the encouragement to his patients of an uninhibited spill-out of the memories, fears, wishes, feelings, thoughts that surged into their minds or pushed through the chinks of consciousness. Freud attended carefully to what his patients said and left unsaid. He noted the emotional content of their words and observed the subtle language of their bodies, too—the sweat, the tensed muscles, the dilated pupils. From these sources Freud came to know more deeply than had before been known the content and nature of anxiety, of conflict, of the rifts that may come between the intellect and the spirit, and of the struggle for power between man's conscious and unconscious selves.

Free association proved to be not only an investigatory tool but also a therapeutic one. By saying aloud what before they had scarcely dared to whisper, by putting into understandable words what had before been experienced only as overpowering feeling, by finding that dreaded thoughts and feelings lost their power when they were exposed to the air and light of discussion, patients found both release and insight. Moreover, they were no longer the passive recipients of a doctor's suggestions but were active participants in their own self-analysis and self-understanding. Along with this a second therapeutic phenomenon occurred. As patients shared with Freud those urges and fears that they had concealed from everyone else, even from themselves, and as they found that he remained uncritical, accepting, dependable, a vital bond of relationship was spun between them. They came to feel at one with their helper and from this therapeutic union to take into themselves their physician's attitude of tolerance and compassion, as well as his verbal suggestions, interpretations, and differing perspectives. Communication was opened in the safety island of relationship.

Social workers have one major tool—that of communication, of the interchange of understanding between people that yields changes of feeling, thought, and action. We took from Freud (not directly from the Viennese analytic couch into the American social agency but through selection and transmutation, bit by bit, over many years) ways by which to transform our once crude communication tools into refined, pliable instruments.

We learned that people disclose what they feel and mean in many ways other than words and that words may be used to conceal as well as to reveal. We learned to shut off our own eagerly racing motors and to attend to the motors of our clients. We learned that, when emotion rides high, reason walks limpingly, that the way to a troubled man's head is through his heart. As the philosopher in the *Crock of Gold* put it, "The head does not hear anything until the heart has listened and what the heart knows today, the head will understand tomorrow."

We learned, further, what we had long known in experience but had scarcely understood: that there are potent powers for good or harm in the relationship between helper and him who needs help; that as people find themselves accepted and warmed by interest and understanding they are freed to move in their thinking and action; and that as they feel at one with that helper they can absorb his unspoken communications of confidence and sustainment and thereby borrow the strength with which to work on their problems.

Thus far, I have spoken chiefly of Freud's contribution to social casework. I have done so because I know this social work process best, and also because Freud's work had its greatest impact upon processes involving individual psychology. However, social work's several other major processes—group work, community organization, administration, and research—have also felt the impact of Freud's works. Today's social group work is concerned not simply with recreational activities, as was once the case, but with the means by which people may develop and exercise their capacities for working and playing together co-operatively. Today's social work administration is a process, not alone of efficient business management, but of "transferring social policy into social services," which combines mechanical means with considerations of the human beings who are the conveyors and those who are the consumers of the services. Community organization turns the good will, social values, and money of the people of the community into organized social services. Social research plays a scrutinizing light, now over people's social needs, and now over the assumptions and practices by which we attempt to meet them.

It is possible that if you were to buttonhole the community chest executive planning his campaign, or a county welfare director worrying over his budgets, or the group leader trying to bring a discussion out of a free-for-all fight, or a researcher pondering his statistics and ask, "How has Freud contributed to what you are doing?" you might be answered with an incredulous stare. Yet, the theory and the practice of these several processes are increasingly influenced by many of Freud's ideas. It is not hard to see why. Administrator, community organizer, group worker, social researcher—all of these work *with* other people, *through* other people, *for* other people. These people, from legislator to file clerk, from board chairman to client, from deacon to delinquent, will function well or ineptly, depending upon their motivations, their feelings, and their being in good communication. These conditions, in turn, depend on the social worker's understanding and appraisal of the irrational as well as the reasonable drives that move people and on relating sensitively to the play of meanings that their words and actions divulge. Furthermore, the values and standards that the community organizer, administrator, and group worker seek to make concrete through social institutions and opportunities are evolving from our new understanding of those conditions of life that are psychologically dwarfing and those that enhance the human personality. These ideas cannot have the elaboration they deserve within the limits of this paper. They merely suggest how Freud's discoveries of the well-springs of human behavior, of the importance of childhood experiences in the formation of personality, of the ways by which communication can vitally influence behavior, have in great degree shaped the concepts, values, and processes of all social work.

One further contribution Freud has made to social work—one less generally recognized than those I have discussed—is the example he unknowingly set as a professional person. Until his later years, Freud worked against great odds. He was derided, attacked, ignored, and, except for the small cluster of his colleagues, he was a lonely man with little status or esteem in the eyes of most of his contemporaries. Social workers, too, perhaps more often than other professional persons, work against heavy odds. Social workers have often experienced in their communities the dubious acceptance, the equivocal status, and the professional loneliness that Freud knew well. The example he set of courage in the face of attack and indifference, his stubborn pursuit of truth, his ability to pour his energies into his studies rather than dissipate them in defensive maneuvers, his ability to bear and surmount isolation and criticism—by these qualities of character and behavior, Freud set a standard for all professional persons.

Genius and creativity cannot be borrowed or even imitated. Its products feed the work of others as the products of Freud's genius expanded social welfare goals and enhanced its practice. For this we acknowledge our great debt to him. However, the attitudes and behavior of another may be learned and incorporated so that they buoy up and enrich the personality of the borrower. This is the additional contribution Freud has made to social work—the exemplification of professional courage, fierce devotion, unassailable integrity. For this unwitting gift, we salute him!

Casework

in

Development

Students of human nature say that one of the marks of personal maturity is to know your full identity—to know what you are made up of, what your place and function in society is, and something of what you must be and do to achieve your goals.

One might say, by analogy, that this is the mark of a profession's maturing too. Fairly young as professions go, social work has been moving swiftly within the last few years to know its special functions and its particular identity. Social casework, which is one of the methods in social work—one of its ways of helping—has been actively engaged in this quest for identity. In agencies, in schools of social work, in clinics and hospitals and wherever case-workers work, they have been asking themselves, "What is our special function? What knowledges and skills are essential to our practice? What are we trying to do for people—cure them? Reorganize their personalities? Arrange them and their lives so that they will be free of future problems? What is our special knowledge and, therefrom, our special responsibility?"

Today we are ready to say what it is and what social

Public Welfare, April 1959, titled "Social Casework Today."

caseworkers do with a clarity and certainty we have not had before. This is because we have come to that point in our maturing when we have achieved a greater sense of wholeness and also a sense of having the wherewithal by which to carry through on our aims.

Caseworkers say that one way by which to know what a person is like today is to examine his yesterdays. So a brief review of social casework's childhood and adolescence may be useful.

Casework's Parentage

The progenitors of casework were a highly respectable lot. They included men and women of education, material well-being, and social conscience—clergymen and lay leaders—citizens concerned with the health, morality, and general well-being of their communities.

The exact parentage of the infant casework is not clear, but it seems to have been mothered by sociology. At least in its infancy it was to sociology that it had its chief attachment and from sociology that it got its chief nurture.

Unemployment, poverty, loss of wages, bad housing, absence of medical care; to all these massive problems students of the social scene called attention. When social agencies were formed to deal with the effects of these problems upon the lives of particular men, women, and children, social casework came into being. It was fed by sociology, though it grew in strength and competence with the exercise of its own muscles.

One day social casework looked at this mother-figure, sociology, in the way that all children one day look at their parents—penetratingly and objectively—and decided that she was something of a frump. She looked increasingly old-fashioned, seemed to have little of interest to say, was endlessly involved in counting dirty linens and rattling cracked statistics. And as casework turned away, uncertainly but rebelliously, it beheld psychiatry. He was a dashing figure—even immoral, some thought at the time—but with much enticing mystery about him and an air of great promise.

It is doubtful that psychiatry was the actual father of casework since he had only recently immigrated to America. But all of casework's filial passions were transferred to and deposited in him. It was an oedipal situation of some clinical interest, in which the mother-figure was rejected and the father-figure was taken on as idol and ego-ideal.

This identification with the father-figure, psychiatry, had a great many growth-producing values for casework. Just as in infancy and early childhood casework had learned much from sociology about the environmental forces that shape men's lives, so now it began to learn from psychiatry about man's "inner environment" and how his personality-forces shape his needs and his external behavior. But it had some drawbacks, too, this oedpial attachment. As often happens in such situations an overdependency developed, and casework lost its sense of its own powers and even of its separate identity. Sometimes it thought of itself only as some kind of extension of this powerful parent-figure, and it hated or at least depreciated those parts of itself that were different from him. This, of course, made for a stormy and uncomfortable adolescence in which there were times when casework doubted itself and clung more closely to the father. Yet, at other times, it thrust out to question and find its selfhood.

In this latter search casework found that while it had learned many things from the parent, psychiatry, the use to which it would put this knowledge had to be self-determined; determined, that is, by casework's sense of its own identity as different and separate from that of either of its parents. This is the happening that marks emergence

87

into adulthood: the knowledge of self as related to others but as a separate and unique entity. At that point one can turn to look at one's forebears with both new interest and new perspective. So when casework turned to look at its mother again, it found, to its surprise, that sociology was flourishing. It was surrounded by an attractive family group, the social sciences, all modishly dressed, worldly in outlook, and able to communicate in thought-provoking ways. Moreover, they were on friendly, at times even intimate, terms with psychiatry.

By one of those flashes of insight (which is really the result of long, unconscious rumination) casework saw that it had had good family connections and good sources of nurture and education. Because of its kinship it had taken into itself knowledge and ideas from both sides of the family. And because of its kinship it was going to be able to be in continuing and ready communication with both sides. As the result of assessing its own life experience and knowing its own strengths, however, it knew that it had a body and stature of its own now, that it had developed ways of acting and resources that were particularly its own, that it could stand on its own two feet and say, "This is what I am; this is what I do; this is what I aim for."

This is not a clinically adequate background history. It has notable omissions and ellipses of both social and psychological forces that have shaped present-day casework. It is, however, a rough explanation of how it is that social casework stands today with its social and psychological knowledge more firmly put together than ever before, with a revitalized interest in its own social purposes and operations.

Seven years ago, in a relatively small meeting in California, the writer urged that caseworkers bend their efforts to "putting the 'social' back into social casework." [1] It was a phrase that caught like wildfire, not

1 Free Association on Problems of Child Welfare," *Child Welfare* 31:7 (July 1952).

because it was so felicitious, but because it expressed what was apparently already smoldering in the minds of social caseworkers across the whole country. It has become almost a shibboleth now. But the fact of which casework can be proud is that in these seven years it has not only faced this challenge but has undertaken in a number of ways to meet it.

Status Today

Here is where casework stands today.

More than ever before it is clear that casework focuses its attention upon the individual (and family) having trouble in carrying one or more of his everyday social tasks. "Everyday social tasks" consist of the responsibilities and operations involved in being and doing something—being and doing the work of a parent, a spouse, a student, a worker. These roles, which all of us carry, contain all the "musts" and "shoulds" and "oughts" of our duties and obligations, and they also contain the rewards and satisfactions and gratifications that come from a sense of working, playing and living in harmonious relationship with other people.

The clients of social casework agencies are people who want or need some help in meeting the expectations or getting the satisfactions in one of these everyday vital social roles. To put this in more familiar terms, they are people who, because of some breakdown in their social situation, some loss of personal resources, or some failure in their own operations, are finding that they cannot cope with some essential life task. This life task may be that of being a parent or of being a wage earner, a family provider, a wife or husband, or even of being somebody's child— because even the role of child carries many requirements of attitude and behavior (although adults often tend to overlook this). Whatever the cause of the problem— whether it lies chiefly in the client's external environment or in his "internal environment," today's caseworker knows that the treatment focus is most validly, most realistically, upon helping his client to achieve greater effectiveness and satisfaction in being and doing what is involved in his social functioning.

There is a balance and honest realism in this focus that is in some contrast to earlier aims of casework. In the early days of psychological naiveté we in casework assumed that if we met certain material needs—by relief, different housing, a new set of foster parents—then we were "curing" the client's malady. We were not infrequently chagrined, however, to find him back at our doors, stubbornly determined to have problems.

In later days of social myopia we assumed that social problems were superficial, even unimportant, and that only the "real problems," that is, the underlying personality problems, were worthy of casework attention. We met frustrations then, too, and among a number of other insights gained was the fact that the expression of emotions and the adventure of self-discovery does not inevitably result in wanting or being able to shoulder the job of being a better parent, spouse, worker, student, or reciprocator in all the varieties of love and work of which life is made up.

Moreover, the fact is that clients come to us asking not that they be "made over" (this is a job for a god, not a caseworker); not that we "cure" or "insure" them against all present and future difficulties (cure is a static illusion in any dynamic conception of life); but simply that we help them to cope with or handle some problems that they are feeling and experiencing right now. They want help to restore their formerly adequate social functioning, to reinforce their current social functioning, or to reform their present circumstances or their ways of dealing with them.

Today's casework has begun to fuse its grasp of

psychodynamics with its emerging understanding of socio-dynamics. The result is the recognition of the tremendous emotional and psychological import of man's daily social experiences. Our knowledge of personality dynamics guides us in how we deal with each different person individually in relation to his problems, and helps us to assess his particular drives and capacities in relation to the problem-solving work he must do. Our understanding of social dynamics—and it is this understanding of which we are now beginning to take full account—focuses casework efforts squarely upon the personality as it is expressed and experienced in its social tasks and social relationships, and further, upon the reality social situation that both bears in upon an individual and is in turn affected by his responses.

What This Implies

As soon as we fully accept the idea that this is our special area of endeavor, a number of consequences ensue. Within them lie some challenges ahead.

We will need to look more penetratingly at the meaning and nature of the social environment of our clients. We sometimes tend to think of environment only as surrounding physical conditions. Actually, however, the most potent social environment with which one interacts is made up of other people—people who threaten or gratify, people who help or who hurt, people who hold power over one or who are dependent upon one's powers, people who give or who take away our sense of adequacy and worth. A factory, a school, a home, and an office are experienced by everyone as good or bad environments first in terms of the human beings who people them—the boss, the teachers, the parents, the co-workers, and the fellow students. It follows from this that casework diagnosis and treatment must of necessity deal not merely with the person who asks for help, the person called the "client," but with the living network of those people with whom he is in vital interaction, whom he affects and by whom he is affected. In large part this is what is implied by the idea of "family diagnosis," an idea that has captured much interest and effort today—the idea that the family is a dynamic network of relationships and that any member does not simply dwell within it, but rather is in continuous interaction with it.

Once upon a time we saw and dealt with marital problems through the person of the complainant on the assumption that if he (though it was usually she) was given understanding of himself, he could eventually manage his relationship with his spouse. Now, and increasingly, we recognize that marriage is a two-way interaction. It involves not only two personalities in relation to one another, but also their expectations of one another and of themselves. We know, then, that we must assess not only one but two personalities; not only two personalities but their socially conditioned ideas as to what is required and desired of each and both in a marriage partnership; not only those ideas, but the ways they act them out. And out of this new complexity of understanding comes changed treatment of marital disharmony, treatment that requires the participation of both partners, since what each feels and thinks and does affects what the marriage is or can be.

So too, there has been a change in our tackling of children's problems. Mother and child were always seen by us as an interacting unit, but only recently have we taken full measure of the father and the part he plays in his child's problem. It is hard to understand why we were so long oblivious to the fact that the father is also a parent (in part, our allegiance to psychiatry's practices was responsible), but now we are convinced that even when the father is for the most part out of the home, the child's life is potently affected by him. A mother's love or excessive indulgence, her hate or subtle rejection of her child, are heavily affected by what her husband is to her as husband and to his child as father. The way a household reorganizes itself when the father enters at six o'clock—the possible shift in its lines of authority, its increased tension or increased pleasantness, its shift from being child-centered to husband-centered—these changes and others are absorbed and reacted to even by very little children. The role the father takes toward the family members—boss, pal, rival, friend-in-need, fire-breathing dragon—this calls up responsive reactions from mother and child.

In short, caseworkers can never again take on the problem of one family member without asking themselves, "Who are the people who constitute this person's living environment? Who, by their attitudes or actions, can be counted on to make or break the working relationship and problem-solving efforts of casework?" These "who's" occur most frequently in the client's family, but they may be found in other situations too, wherever one person is in some meaningful interaction with another, especially in relation to his problem.

Importance of Others

Now we in casework have always said that environmental manipulation was one of our treatment means. But is it not true that we long tended to think of it as making arrangements for our clients, as shifting the scenes, so to speak, or bringing new properties onto the stage of their living? And in the period of immersion in the client's inner workings is it not true that we assured ourselves that given relief of emotional stress and self-understanding the client would somehow be able to "adjust" to his environment or change it by himself? What the growing synthesis of psychological and social understanding makes clear is that the everyday people in our client's everyday life continuously affect what he feels, thinks, and does, and that in order to influence his ways of feeling and acting we must not only understand his living environment but move out into it to work directly with those persons who are involved in his problems or their solutions. An environment that consists of people will not be "manipulated." It calls for all the psychological insights and therapeutic skills at our command, nothing less than is involved in the one-to-one interview with the main client. It calls for greater skill, actually, than we have developed as yet, because involved here are considerations of how to interview several persons at one time; of how to motivate people to use themselves in the interests of others; of how to achieve some balance between the simultaneous and often conflicting wants and needs of several people. These are no easy tasks.

A recent study presents some cogent facts as to how vital this effort is. The Research Center of the University of Chicago's school of social work has completed a study of more than 300 cases to find out what makes clients quit or continue with agency treatment. Among a number of interesting findings are these: those clients who brought problems of interpersonal difficulties (marital and parent-child conflicts, chiefly) tended to continue to work with the agency when other people in their lives were supportive rather than undermining. Conversely, if the role played by other people in their lives was impeding they tended to drop out of service.[2] The challenge inherent in these findings is clear.

In no sense does this suggest that we in casework can overlook that environment with which social work has continuously been concerned—that of the social conditions that enrich or impoverish human living. In our early days these were the environmental factors that we "manipulated." A whole sector of social casework turned its eyes

---

2 Lilian Ripple, "Factors Associated with Continuance in Casework Service," *Social Work* 2 (January 1957).

away from these environmental problems when mass need began to be met by public assistance and insurance programs and when, by chronological coincidence, the problems in man's inner environment captured our interest. Today, our fusing social and psychological understanding lights up anew how vital are the mundane floorboards of man's life for the promotion of his essential welfare and the prevention of his disorganization.

"Prevention" is in the mind and on the tongue of everyone who is today concerned with community welfare—prevention of the warped personalities, the perverted behavior, the human wastage and suffering that every day's newspaper recounts. Prevention is easier said than done. It requires an all-out effort that would need to involve every professional, political, and economic institution in any community. Social casework can tackle only its small part, but it may be a significant part.

Environment and Personality

To the social caseworker come people who are already in trouble, already suffering from physical, social, and psychological stresses. So caseworkers will always have to work first with repairing the damage done to people and with reinforcing their precarious social functioning. The ounce of prevention is contained within these tasks. It lies in this fact: there is no personality problem, no inner conflict, no apathy, hostility, shiftlessness, or guilt with which the person was born. A person's problems of inner disturbance were once borne in upon him from the outside. On one day of his life some external event, something in his external environment, drove deep into him and wrenched his inner being. Or, more commonly, over many days and months in his formative years certain social conditions or social relationships hurt or frustrated him repeatedly or chronically so that he was left feeling corroded, less than a whole person, or filled to the brim with unmanageable emotions.

There is repeated and reliable evidence that environmental deprivations—the lack of the means by which we feel secure, or decent, or equal to other people—may contribute heavily to warping the personality or exciting explosive emotions. Only as the social caseworker, social agencies, and planning councils take full note of the conditions and circumstances in the external environment that shape and color the internal environment, only then will they fully grasp the preventive import—or the physical, social, and mental hygiene import—of the everyday, undramatic social services and resources that are provided, or should be provided.

The Chicago study mentioned above produces some facts on this subject too. It was found that clients who brought environmental problems to the family agency (and these more often than not were accompanied by psychological problems) tended to continue to work with the agency in significant numbers when there was indication that their environmental problems were subject to change. Conversely, if it seemed that nothing would or could be done about the concrete problem they presented, they dropped out of work with the agency. These facts speak for the continuing concern the social caseworker and casework agency must maintain that bread and butter resources be available for bread and butter needs.

Finally—(this is "finally" only because space does not permit a complete accounting of the new tasks in which social casework is involved)—finally, it is a mark of casework's maturing that it is turning again to study and extend its helping services to individuals and families who, because of their standards and actions, are at odds with the social community. They have variously been called the "hard-core," the "hard-to-reach," the "multiple-problem" families. Their common characteristic is that despite their being beset by problems of health, money, internal strife, and family disorganization, they want nothing of social work help. Yet, because they breed unhappy, sick, and sometimes delinquent children they are a thorn in the community well-being.

In our early days we were much involved with such families, believing, in the tradition of social Darwinism, that if we could change the environmental conditions to which they were subjected we could automatically change them. But we found to our repeated dismay that change in human beings was dependent upon their wish and will to change and not upon superimposed external arrangements. So we turned away from these social outcasts and toward those people who both wanted help with their problems and could engage themselves in working on them. Simultaneously we turned to psychiatry to learn about people's inner workings. As we came to understand something of the mysteries of people's inner drives and motives and resistances, we began to consider the possibility that there might be ways of helping people to want help, ways of stimulating people to want to change their standards and modes of behavior. Indeed, some caseworkers even wondered if it was the agencies themselves that had become "hard-to-reach" since many of them remained aloof from all but "treatable" clients.

Combined Approach

Now again these insights about human motivation have joined with revivified social concerns. In a number of places about the country caseworkers are leaving the relative comfort and security of their offices to beat the pavements, to climb rickety stairs, to try to get one foot into suspiciously held doors, to see whether, when psychological understanding and skill are combined with social concern, people can be helped to want help, especially for their children's welfare.

There are many problems that this work with the unwilling client raises. It is time-consuming and therefore costly to the community. It is energy consuming and therefore costly to the caseworker. Perhaps in the end it will require the longevity of a Methuselah, the patience of a Job, and the wisdom of a Solomon to carry it through successfully. Meantime, casework has undertaken it as another challenge to its developing skills and constant aims.

These, then, are a few of the ways in which casework is demonstrating its coming of age. It is clear as to what it is. It is a way in social work by which people are helped to cope with the problems they encounter in their functioning as social beings, and by which to enhance people's desire, ability, and opportunity to carry their daily life tasks with competence and satisfaction. When this goal is plainly seen, all casework's methods of social and psychological influence may be bent to its achievement. Growing knowledge of man as a social as well as psychological and physical being infuses the "how" of casework's doing with new perspectives on the "what" and the "why."

Sometimes it seems that the word "challenge" is a euphemism for "impossible job." There are many challenges and many very difficult, if not impossible, jobs ahead of us before we can say with honesty and satisfaction that we have achieved our goals. But there remains a further mark of maturity; that is to come to grips with the fact that in the life of a profession, as in the life of a man, the rewards lie less often in full achievement and more often in the stretch and growth of muscle, mind, and spirit as we doggedly strive toward it.

Social Work Method:
A Review of the
Decade 1955–65

A review should be done in a period of tranquility, with things settled down, at some place of distance from that which is being observed and analyzed in order to get perspective and to see patterns. If these are necessary conditions, this review of social work method is done under the worst of circumstances. Perhaps in no previous span of ten years have there been so much surge and change in social work, so many forays into new areas of action and thought as in this past decade. Armies of caseworkers shift from individual to group treatment, group workers shift from socialization to therapeutic activity, community workers split into phalanxes of "developers," "planners," "organizers." Everyone's banners cry "onward!" or "unity!" And in this melee of surge and sound the writer scrambles about, an overstimulated, underequipped observer trying to see where social work methods are today.

This introduction is my confession that I have not been able to find a coherent framework within which to view methodological trends in the past ten years. I have talked to practitioners and to teachers, reviewed the literature, twisted and turned my sights. The one certainty I have

Social Work, October 1965, titled "Social Work Method: A Review of the Past Decade."

captured is that of uncertainity, of change, movement, fluidity, and breakthrough. It is said that in some sciences knowledge doubles every ten years. I do not think social work's knowledge has doubled in this past decade. But it is clear that its push to know, its efforts to explore knowledge, its self-demanding aspirations for extending, identifying, organizing, and testing its functions and its practices have proceeded by geometric leaps. I do not presume to know whether this is good or bad, whether it is a situation for professional self-congratulation or for viewing with alarm. All I can promise is that what follows is one social worker's willingness to share a view of kaleidoscopic movement in social work's modes of action, in its three major methods of intervention: casework, group work, and community organization.

First I invite you to listen to the changing vocabulary of social work. The thrust is from passive to active voice, from past imperfect to present imperative tense, from ideas of adjustment to those of coping, from social workers as enablers to social workers as change agents, from client as having self-determination to client as change target, from compromise to manipulation of power, from co-ordination to innovation. I do not mean that all these are antithetical ideas or that in other guises they have not figured in social work considerations before. But words have consequences and the emphasis on the aggressive, innovative, intrusive mode is strong among us now; it reveals our press and inclination.

Changes in Casework

The surge of new ideas, the shift of focus, the play of new approaches are many and plain to be seen in the method called "casework." Even a superficial glance will reveal these movements—some of them trends, some merely oscillations. There has been a shift in theory framework—

from id to ego psychology. The caseworker's attention is increasingly on the nature and efficacy of the individual's conscious and just-preconscious behaviors, on the mechanisms by which he protects, adapts, or copes with both the internal and external stresses he encounters. Those functions of the ego that have to do with perception and cognition and interpersonal competence, those feelings that have to do with motivation for change, those interactions between self and object that are called "social functioning"—these are increasingly in the center of casework's study and influence efforts. Consonant with this (whether as cause or consequence or both it is hard to know) is a shift from focus on intrapersonal conflict to focus on conflicts in interpersonal transactions, from person viewed against the background of past and in the central spotlight, center stage, to person viewed as part of an interacting role network in which he is both acted upon and acting, both being and becoming.

Underpinning these new perspectives are certain expanding concepts from the theory of what we call "social science." Perhaps "science" is a euphemistic appellation, promising more than it can give surety for—but more of this later. At present, by whatever name, the theory and findings of person-to-group in a transaction are base-points for change in casework's focus and treatment methods. Family structure and interplay, culture and class norms as behavior determinants—these, among other ideas, permeate the caseworker's office talk at the least and his thinking and experimental action at the most responsible level.

Related to this focus on person-in-social-functioning (whether "social" is defined as one person in interaction with one other or as one person in that amorphous organism called society) is the upsurge of interest in the poor and the culture of poverty. The psychodynamic impact of long and chronic impoverishment, the culture of social work itself and the acculturation of its practitioners, questions of where casework comes in or gets off in the sudden popular espousal of the cause of the now all-too-visible poor—all these figure with new prominence in casework discussion. It was one segment of casework that provided the first professionalized push toward the poor before they became the darlings of the press and politics. In spots across the country casework experiments were being tried early in the fifties to reach the hard-to-reach, to plan what are now called "intervention strategies" but what were then called aggressive or assertive efforts to motivate the unmotivated, to socialize the socially disorganized and unwilling clients of courts or family and child welfare agencies. As these efforts were made and as difficulties were encountered they served to raise many still unanswered questions in casework about the aptness and applicability of the traditional casework model for the needful but inarticulate, apathetic, or openly resistive population.

Partly rising out of these questions and experiences, partly stimulated by concurrent public health mental health action researches, there have poured into casework ideas of crisis treatment and prevention. These ideas, too, challenge the traditional casework treatment model. And they challenge the structure and programs of many agencies that use casework as their major mode of problem-solving. Concepts of crisis or of prevention, when they are understood in depth, push for redefinitions of both casework means and ends. They require rethinking of casework's ideas of what is to be diagnosed and what is to be treated and what treatment consists of. They tie in with a firm grasp of ego psychology, with many social science insights, with poverty problems and manpower shortages. Thus one sees a whole network of recognized and/or unnoted connections pushing and shoving at the formerly orderly method of operation called casework.

But we are not yet done. Manpower shortages in

casework combined with fragments of social science ideas about socialization, reference groups, role networks, therapeutic milieus, family transactional and communication systems have somehow coalesced in an uneasy combination to create a major methodological shift. Reference here is to the phenomenon of work with groups by caseworkers everywhere—in family and child welfare agencies, residential centers, psychiatric and general hospitals and clinics. Purposes of work with groups range from information-conveyance to decision-making to therapy, in numbers varying from the dyad of a marital problem to the triad of an oedipal problem to the octet (or more) of strangers gathered together about some problem common to them all. Indeed, the use of group interviewing by caseworkers seems to have risen to fad dimensions and the caseworker who does not carry at least one group is just plainly out of style. (Or perhaps he is in the next decade's avant-garde!)

Casework's Use of Groups. The use of group session by caseworkers has had many spokesmen in casework's literature and many values attributed to it as a substitute for, or as a supplementary method to, the one-to-one interview. These attributed values range from expedience and economy of time and effort to the connections assumed to exist between the group process and ego support, between group participation and facilitated social functioning, between enhanced communication and enhanced happiness. (Someone should say something about the possibility that there are some things in interpersonal life that are better uncommunicated either by word or action. It is *what* is communicated, not alone the phenomenon of communication, that is our treatment concern.)

No one can deny that there exists an association between and among these phenomena. But there have been as yet few attempts to articulate and test what the explicit connections are. In what ways, for example, does ego

103

psychology relate to the use of group interviewing? What different purposes are served by group interviewing from those served by individual interviews? What different expectations in terms, for example, of relationship to the caseworker, of client's self-understanding versus, say, his self-management? For what sorts of problems is the individual best dealt with in the group? Should the decision to use one-to-one or one-to-group interviewing be made in relation to problem type or in relation to goal? In short, in casework's rather sanguine taking on of group interviews there is roused a beehive of questions yet to be asked and answered.

Caseworkers writing on the use of groups do not seem troubled about group dynamics or group process in their difference from the one-to-one interview. Questions such as what is the nature of "groupness," what principles govern the social worker's relative activity or passivity in the group, what techniques further intercommunication among group members rather than dialogues held with the caseworker in the presence of others—these and like questions have not seemed to plague caseworkers to the same degree or extent that questions about principles of individual interviewing plague group workers who are moving in casework's direction. "Group process" is called by name in casework writings. But what this process is and what group dynamics are as differentiated from individual dynamics have yet to be identified and grappled with.

Certainly at the points when the caseworker takes on a group and the group worker lifts out single members from his group for individual interviews differences in methods grow blurred. Perhaps this presages a merging and integration of the methods of casework and group work. Certainly it requires further work at what is already taking place in a number of schools of social work across the country: examination of the specific and generic elements in each method, looking toward possible combinations.

104

Because we sometimes lose sight of the obvious it is here pointed up: the likeness between casework and group work at levels of commitment, conviction, and knowledge of man and society are easily seen and affirmed. But it is the knowledge of transactional processes and the means by which these are managed—the know-how and skill of *doing*, the differences between interviewing one-to-one and one-to-group, the principles that govern what is done and how it is done—these have yet to be explored and articulated so that we can know what makes casework and group work alike and also different.

The Thrust of Research. Of the many changes to be seen in the casework method over the past ten years space here permits lifting out only one more—the remarkable thrust of research in this practice method. Prior to this decade, research in social work had focused chiefly on the nature of social problems and agency operations. Within the past ten years some outstanding researches have focused on the casework method—that is, on the relation between what the practitioner does and its outcome. The shifts in the research microscope's focus are not our story here. What is of import is the fact that research in a process or method can come about only when there is established a firm base of regularities of practice. Regularities rise up out of practice that has been conceptualized and to some extent systematized. Casework, for a number of reasons, is the social work method that has most fully explicated and organized its practice rationale. This is what has readied its practice for testing and research scrutiny and, further, this is what gives its practitioners the courage—for it takes courage—to open up their practice to critical study.

Impact of Social Science Theory. The impact of social science theory on casework is plain to see. Because the problem of its absorption and use in practice is the same for the several methods, it will be dealt with later. Here it need only be noted that concepts such as role, class, reference group—that place and explain the individual in his social context—have been used in casework for expanding its diagnostic understanding. But the use of such understanding for treatment actions is not as yet clearly manifest. The question is whether we are nursing an illusion to the effect that understanding a problem in different perspectives really tells us what to do and how to do it. Does the incorporation of social science content into casework—or group work or community work—contribute to the development of our skills and techniques, to the processes by which we attempt to effect change?

Changes in Group Work

When we turn to group work we see that it, too, is in rapid movement, undergoing almost revolutionary changes. It has burst the too-narrow seams of its basketball uniforms and arts-and-crafts smocks; increasingly it appears in the contrasting symbolic garments that bespeak the poles of its present scope—the authority-cool white coats of hospital and clinical personnel and the play-it-cool windbreaker of the street corner gang-worker.

The past decade's changes in group work are changes in its territorial domains, in the problems it considers to be amenable to its skills, and in its modes of action. Its domain has widened from agencies for youth development, character-building, leisure-time activities—the activities focused on enhancement of social functioning and enrichment of opportunities—to include those agencies and places that are set up to rehabilitate or restore or reform such social functioning as is held to be problematic, impaired, deficient. It has taken on the problems of malfunctioning of the individual as they are manifest in his alienation from groups or in his interpersonal—which is to say his "group"—transactions. It has extended its repertoire of professional actions to include a range of therapeutic methods of influence. From the moment of its professionalization group work sought to identify and "diagnose" the individual members of groups. In this sense group work always individualized. But the actual treatment of the individual group member for his particular problems and the relation of such treatment of personal problems to group membership and process—these are in the center of group work concerns today.

As group work has been introduced and has proved useful in psychiatric and other rehabilitative centers it has inevitably become infused with ideas of therapeutic milieu, of individual psychopathology and psychodynamics (as they are expressed and affected by the group), and even with the study-diagnosis-treatment model that casework inherited (with some chronically awkward consequences) from those same settings. At the risk of oversimplification it may be said that at one of its surging edges group work is increasingly involved with the persons, places, problems, and even some of the processes that not too long ago were assumed to "belong" to casework.

Reaching Out to the Hard-to-Reach. But there are bents in other directions too, tugs by forces both within and outside social work. Group work actually never left the neighborhood house, never left the disinherited population. Yet, the influence of the settlement house waned as house residents "settled" but populations moved, and neighborhood houses sometimes found themselves, by urban rot or renewal, bereft of a neighborhood. Moreover, the gap between social work and the poor grew wider as social workers struggled for professional status, for clients who were "in" members of the community, who were approachable, accessible, understandable. Within the past decade, owing in part to the new respectability of the poor, in part to conscience-nudgers within its own ranks, group work, like casework, has turned again to work with the most needful, to reverse what Vinter called the "retreat from those most in need." Infused now with new insights about the effects of social class, culture, ethnicity, upon the motivations and communications of the long-poor and long-outcast, one sector of group work has turned afresh to attempting to engage the disengaged, the alienated, the delinquency-prone young people in today's slums.

Paralleling casework's reaching out to the hard-to-reach, group work has stepped up its reaching out in hitherto untried ways to the hard-to-engage youth. Delinquents or potential delinquents, socially alienated or socially threatening gang groups, young people who have "dropped out" not only from school but from all regularized, socially valued roles—these are again in the practice concerns of group work and at the growing edge of its experiments. These groups are problematic in more ways than one. To work with them requires creative synthesis of both sociodynamic and psychodynamic knowledge and particular awareness and management of the gap that exists between the values and norms of the socially alienated and those of social work. Moreover, such dual perceptions and management require security and free-wheeling capacity in the group worker. He must often be "detached" from an agency and all its security appurte-nances and at the same time remain "attached" to professional values; at the same time he must become "attachable" to the distrustful, uncommunicative, often antagonistic persons who are his potential clients. This is no small task.

Problem of Self-Definition. When one looks at this range of practice embraced by group work it is easy to understand the run of high feeling in its ranks about its definition and identity and the push by its leaders and formulators to develop further its practice models and principles. In the examination of its writings one sees some internecine struggles over whether its major commitments should be on the continuum of education-to-therapy or on the continuum of education-to-socialization. And sometimes these issues and questions are made murky by confusing personalities with positions.

Nomenclature and the meanings that are contained in names are in the center of group work discussions. What is "group work" to "group counseling" to "group therapy" to "group dynamics" to "group process"? The echoes of like questions in casework sound fainter now than they did ten years ago, it may hearten group workers to know. It is not that questions such as where casework leaves off and psychotherapy begins have been resolved neatly. Rather it is that there has been some acceptance of the fact that there are more ways to help people than we have dreamed of. It is that perhaps the questions of boundaries are far less important than the questions of whether we can indeed translate professional purpose into such practice and service as will meet not categories of method but client-need.

Awareness of Individual Psychology. Add to its self-definition and identity struggles the new awareness in group work of individual psychology, of the relatedness between intrapersonal needs and interpersonal behavior. Increasingly interested in the individuals who make up the group and concerned with how to deal with them individually when this seems called for, group workers look toward casework's area of special knowledge and technique. One gets the impression that somehow group workers are more respectful and tentative in their approach to working with individuals than are caseworkers in their approach to the group. One reason probably is that as group workers approach treatment of the individual they do so because of his sickness or malfunctioning; this is uneasy ground. On the other hand, as caseworkers approach the group, they move into what seems, on the surface at least, to be a diluted, safety-in-numbers situation. Whatever the causes, group work is involved in the effort to incorporate more fully and firmly into its methodology the knowledge of how to deal with the individual person who from time to time may need to be lifted out of group sessions into the one-to-one encounter.

It would be a service to all social work methods if group work did not too immediately and slavishly imitate the casework model; if, rather, it asked and answered some questions of its own. Its use and patterning of the individual interview, for example, might be shaped by such questions as the following: the relation between what is done in the individual interview to the purpose for which the person is being kept in the group, the effect on the relationship between group worker and other members of his group when one member has been taken on for special treatment; at a more theoretical level the connections between those social science concepts that have long underpinned the group work method and the concepts of individual psychodynamics that are coming to have increasing play in group work thinking, and the connections between both these bodies of theory and the group process by which planned change can be made to occur. What is suggested is that group work's present thinking on its problems of method development and practice theory might serve all three social work methods if it did not too quickly surrender its uniqueness for the comfort of prefabricated action principles of another method.

On one of its pushing-out edges of practice, then, group work is increasingly overlapping with the casework method. At its opposite frontier it overlaps with community work. The boundaries between group work and community organization have always been fluid and close. With the renewed interest in settlement house activities and the experiments by group workers in moving out into the community for the redirection and reorganization of indigenous groups there is a growing common ground. So we turn to look at the community organization method, the third of social work's major practice methods.

Changes in Community Work

Perhaps the community organization method epitomizes the changes and conflicts in social work practice today. Its methodological struggles and its pressing questions may be seen as heightened versions of theory and practice problems in casework and group work.

To begin with, it is not simply a rhetorical question to ask, "What is community organization?" The *Social Work Yearbook, 1957* contains one article on community organization.[1] The 1965 *Encyclopedia of Social Work* carries three articles on three different but manifestly interrelated areas of community work: "Community Development," "Community Organization," and "Community Planning and Development."[2] The author of "Community Development"—a term lucky enough to have the identifying stamp of "international usage" on it—points to the problems inherent and unresolved in differentiating these three branch-outs from what had been considered a practice unity. For purposes of simplicity an embracing name and one that ties in most readily with casework and group work will be used here: "community work."

Viewed from the vantage point of interested ignorance, the thrust in community work, like those in casework and group work, is a response both to internal and external stimuli that made existent boundaries too tight and old roles too limiting. The external stimuli are those that have

1 Campbell G. Murphy, "Community Organization for Social Welfare," in *Social Work Year Book, 1957* ed. Russell H. Kurtz (New York: National Association of Social Workers, 1957). pp. 179–85.
2 Charles E. Hendry, "Community Development," Meyer Schwartz, "Community Organization," and Jack Stumpf, "Community Planning and Development," in *Encyclopedia of Social Work,* ed. Harry L. Lurie (New York: National Association of Social Workers, 1965), pp. 170–208.

become commonplace in the daily lives of all our citizenry: challenges to develop ideas, plans, programs, policies, new structures, new "targets" for coping with economic, educational, and cultural poverty and for socially alienated and socially antagonistic groups.

The idea of the "Great Society," the opening of federal concern and coffers for the creation and management of new programs for social welfare, the self-assertion and active organization of those sectors of society that for years had been depressed and silent—these are all-but-revolutionary upheavals. Suddenly social work finds that the intents and resources it had long called for are almost to be had. Amost to be had—not for the asking, but for the invention and presentation of bold, imaginative programs, preferably those that come with how-to-do-it directions. This is a major challenge to community workers. Add to this the widespread rise of vigorous young leaders at universities, in churches, in grass roots (or perhaps one should say instead "street pavement") organizations—all of whom are organizing, advocating, researching, and giving service—and the position and functions of the professional community worker are jostled as well as challenged.

The shift, then, seems to be from community organization as a method that has largely, although never exclusively, been involved in the co-ordination of existing services to the development of new kinds of structures and functions; from the redistribution of voluntary funds to the invention of programs and structure that can fruitfully utilize the millions of tax dollars that are ready to be poured into social welfare programs; from the concept of "citizen participation" that identified "citizen" in Platonic terms as one of the élite, one held to be "fit" to govern, to the concept of citizen participation as including those who are assumed to be the beneficiaries of service, now viewed as potential "indigenous leaders"; from consultation and standard-setting functions to social planning and action functions; from a sense of "community" as a small, stable, circumscribed unit to a recognition of the open and broken and expanding boundaries of present-day communities; and finally to awareness that "community" is a concept that demands a new definition and vision. Thus the social work method called community organization, which has in the past largely suggested a replenishment and tidying-up within a bounded area of given circumstances and conditions, has stretched and opened to include concepts of community development and planning and action, all with progressive, participant connotations.

The author of "Community Planning and Development" lists twenty-two "central issues" as yet unresolved in community work. They are questions far more upsetting to the equilibrium of its practitioners and those that alternately nettle and excite group work and casework, questions that express some of the paradoxes inherent in the traditional model of this method.

Persons, Problems, and Place. Who, for example, is the client of the community worker? Many community workers reject the use of that designation completely because of its connotation of dependency. But even if one uses it in its more general sense, as meaning "one who employs the services of a profession," who is the client? What group of persons make up the client-system of the community worker? Is it those who hire him or those for whose supposed benefit he is hired?

In the event of conflict of interest, with whose side is he allied—with those who employ him or those whom he is supposed to help? Put crudely: in a power struggle between opposing forces in a community, a militant neighborhood council, let us say, and the governing board of the neighborhood house that originally gave encouragement and house-room and a community worker to aid "indigenous participation," with whom will the community worker align himself?

For the community worker who is a professional social worker, what problems are most appropriate? Among the galaxy of social welfare problems and programs—the restitutive needs, the co-ordinating necessities, the social policy-making, the planning and engineering of action programs, the organization and support of voluntary efforts—which among these ought to be the priority or ascendant concerns of the community workers? Does this decision relate to power or skill or auspice?

What is the place, the auspice that hires the professional community worker? As long as community work remained within the safe boundaries of organized chests and council agencies it was in the ordered, relatively comfortable position of its sibling methods, casework and group work, shaped and channeled by its sponsorship. With its sallying forth into new areas and ventures it steps off from its familiar floorboards, with some gain in a heady sense of freedom but some loss of backing and certainty. Goals, structures, and functions are "set" by the setting in which the social worker is employed. So, too, are the worker's ways of working, his actions toward change. As he becomes the organizer of a new kind of community service, for example, a community mental health center for which patterns are only now in the making, what does he do, with and for whom, and by what methods?

These questions of problems-to-be-worked, persons-to-be-worked-with, and place all bear on process and on social work values as well. Power as a social force has pushed its way into frank and uneasy recognition by community workers. Power structures, power conflicts, power play are considerations that must be in the very center of any community-wide intervention strategy, whether political, economic, or social. The social scientist offers ways by which power phenomena can be understood and even manipulated. But between understanding and manipulation lie the considerations of professional ethics and human relationships. The social worker's pause to weigh and choose among relative values may become both his glory and his bane.

Turn to the Social Sciences. Perhaps even more than in casework and group work, community work has turned in this past decade to the social sciences for illumination. The findings of social science may have particular relevance for community work because they are so often focused on the large social scene and on its systems and trends. Power structure and dynamics, bureaucracy and its workings, the idea of social systems, these constructs and others are both underpinning community practice and shaking it up. New dimensions of goal and tasks are revealed by new knowledge. But, as has been said for casework and group work, this expanded and deepened understanding has not yet flashed directional arrows that point to what to do and how to do it. Community work has yet to coax out of its knowledge the principles that will guide its special actions.

Defining the Method. Within the past few years faculties of schools of social work, individually and in concert under the aegis of the Council on Social Work Education, the National Association of Social Workers through its productive commissions and committees, and groups of community workers on their own have taken on and wrestled with the problems of defining and delineating the methods called "community organization" or "community action," of identifying its special social work characteristics, and especially of trying to extract and name its particular techniques. If it is to be taught in schools of social work its content must be clarified and its "strategies of intervention" must be cast into some systematic organized form. On the one side lies the danger that in the eagerness to find likeness among social work methods community work might be pushed and stuffed into treatment models that do not suit its specialness. On the other side lies the danger of ambiguity masquerading as flexibility.

Furthermore, the student of community work may be

given little or no training in the depth experience of the one-to-one or one-to-small-group encounter and problem-solving that has been held to be the nucleus of social work learning. It is possible that such direct work with the people who actually suffer the problems with which social work is concerned is the crucial experience that results in the vital and telling difference between a bright young sociologist who enters community work and an equally bright young social worker who adds to his brightness and youngness a feelingful knowledge of the emotional and personal impact of social problems. These educational considerations and many others lie ahead for those who look to the development of community work.

Because community work is the most complex among the social work methods, because its operations are far more variegated and far less subject to worker control than those involved in casework or group work, and because it is currently in a phase of redefinitions and new insights, the probability is that its operational theory will be some time in developing.

Development of Practice Theory

All three social work methods—casework, group work, and community work—thus have as their major task ahead the development of their practice theory, the theory that explains and guides their action. What the social worker does and how he does it—this is what will spell the special identity of the social work profession. We are surely and even rapidly adding to our store of knowledge; we have given tongue and heart to what we believe in and hold to be good; but the what and the how of carrying knowledge and belief into action—these are yet to be formulated. And this is difficult. Among the many problems that rise up as soon as one speaks of "method" are two that merit some further comment. One is that of the uses of social science.

The other is that of whether social work methods are more alike than different from one another, more generic than specific, or the other way around.

Part of the problem in the actual use of social science theory for action purposes is not in the theory but in ourselves. Our difficulty is our overwhelming sense of needfulness—the feeling that somehow we have failed to find the keys that unlock the right doors to human behavior. This combines with the hope that someone else holds these keys. Once we thought sociology held them; then we thought psychoanalytic theory held them; now we seem to think social science holds them. We are not even sure what social science consists of, what combined bodies of knowledge are its constituents and whether all of these bodies can claim the rubric "science." But we reach out avidly, eager to know better in order to do better.

The caveat we must hold before ourselves is against letting the need blind us. Words seem to hold magic, and the use of words like "communication" and "transaction" and "client-system" and "role network" may infuse us with a heady sense of having something to conjure with. We can weave word-spells around one another, but unless we plumb these words for their particular meaning, for what phenomena they express, and then for what their implications for action are, we will find ourselves disappointed again that what we thought was gold is dross. Something of this sort has begun to happen in work on family diagnosis. It somehow does not quite tell us what to do about family treatment. We have a whole bagful of new words with their attendant manifest meanings by which to talk about family organization and processes, but we have yet to distill from those words their implications for treatment actions. We might even find, if we look hard, that we have some throwaways among them.

Furthermore, what is called social science is not all of a piece. It is not a nice, unified system; it ranges across varied phenomena in a vast field. Naturally, then, it holds contradictory findings and hypotheses, and many empty spaces, too. We will not find complete coherence in social science concepts and theory; moreover we must recognize that its findings are not of equal import to us. Some of its knowledge is more and some less useful to our purposes. Some ideas relate more closely to one method in social work than to another. It is our particular and identified practice problem that should determine what we look for in any body of knowledge, social science or any other. Selectively based on our knowledge of what we are after, what we lack, what we need to understand, and on the relevance or fit of any given bit of knowledge for our work—this is our necessity.

Finally, the most difficult problem in the incorporation of social science into social work method is the problem of translating what is understood into principles of action. One of the major differences between social science theory and psychodynamic theory is that the latter, whether orthodox or heterodox, is derived from action, from efforts at intervention in psychological processes. Psychoanalysis started as research but turned out to be a therapeutic process. Psychodynamic theory has been elaborated and extended, to be sure, by speculation, extrapolation, experiment and literary and dramatic analogies. But basically it is a practice theory, continuously tested in a process of transactions between a treating person and his patient or client. This is why psychodynamic theory so readily yields up practice principles, why it is so readily translatable into guides for doing. Doing reveals dynamics. (This is probably one reason why casework's development of its practice theory came earlier and more easily than that of other social work methods.) Psychodynamic theory is chiefly, though not completely, based on actual intervention. Social science theory is chiefly, though not completely, based on study that yields explanations.

Social science has studied and sought to explain the existence of social phenomena, to measure their frequency, extent, and regularity, and to postulate cause-effect relationships. The units studied have been large so that quantification would support generalization. With some notable exceptions in action programs, the researcher has been an objective observer of what was being studied, outside the process, dedicated to avoiding such interventions or action as might change the nature of what was being studied. Thus, there is an understandable gap between social science findings and their applicability to social work actions. Treatment or intervention strategies do not freely flow out of these findings. Whatever action guides they hold have to be teased out and translated into action terms.

The further probability is that for the most part it will take action to produce action theory. Description and study of practice, its regularities, the relation between what the social worker does and what happens—these operations in social work's several methods will need to be scrutinized, identified, formulated, and connected. In short, we shall probably have to search at our own doorsteps for the principles that explain what and how we do.

The second problem in method formulation today is that in our eagerness for "togetherness" and in the battering push on schools of social work to prepare versatile social workers, not narrow technicians, we may too quickly crystallize and box in our methods. This problem deserves a paper on its own; here it can only be touched.

Need for Diversity in Methods

At a high level of generalization it is easy to see a common pattern in casework, group work, and community work. For all of them there is a generic, that is, an inclusive or general base. This consists of our knowledge of man in society, of social welfare programs and purposes, of our values and ethical commitments, and of our problem-solving process that follows the logic of identification of the problem-to-be-worked, its study, its assessment, and the making of decisions and choices about modes of action. But all this offers only the most general outlines of practice. At the moment of going into action—at the moment when a live social worker engages himself with his live client—whether that client is one person, a group, or interacting groups—for the purpose of changing behavior or conditions, then his method becomes specific, particular, differentially shaped, and acted out. The ways a social worker translates his understandings into actions, how he handles himself and the people and circumstances he aims to change—these constitute his technical know-how. It is this know-how that needs to be named, explained, and regularized.

The danger is that in our effort to find social work "all of a piece" we may try too quickly and too hard to push and fit new, emergent, as yet insufficiently tried modes of practice into established or old molds. And we may lose, thereby, the richness and potentialities of diversity in practice.

One sees, for example, a continued eyeing of casework for its fairly neat array of action principles. Sometimes that eyeing is admiring. It says, "How orderly you are. We too can fit into your scheme." Sometimes that eyeing is baleful. It says, "What a poor scheme you work by. It doesn't provide a hint about social reform or prevention." Both positions are in error. The casework model is a clinical model. It is focused on clear and present mal-functioning in single units of person or family. Its purpose is to give help when such an individual unit experiences and feels present problems. Its actions are founded on conceptions of the motivating powers within individuals and how those powers are enhanced by relationship, on notions of the releasing and reorganizing values of identifications, of talk, of emotional expression followed by reflective consideration, and so on. As a clinical model it has validity. For certain persons with certain problems this one-to-one model cannot readily be disposed of.

On the other hand, when casework moves into dealing with other sorts of problems—for example, those of crisis situations—and with certain kinds of people—for example, the socially antagonistic and alienated—and with new sorts of goals—for example, that of prevention—its clinical model may well need radical change. This change needs to occur, for instance, when caseworkers begin to group their clients as is the trend today. What assumptions are they making about the nature of relationship in the twosome, about group members as sources of supplementary ego supports, and so forth? In short, the clinical treatment model cannot simply be extended to embrace other kinds of units and ends; on the other hand, it should not be held wanting because it does not shape treatment actions for which it was never intended.

If this need for working out differentiated treatment models based on differentiated persons, purposes, and programs holds within one method, casework, it suggests that among the three social work methods even greater diversity may be needed and found. We should not too readily expect that our action theory will neatly fall into the same molds for all three methods. Perhaps we should ask ourselves in what ways an action model for therapeutic purposes is likely to differ from one that has educational purposes, and this model from one that has planning-prevention purposes. Maybe the way to go about identifying social work practice activities is not within the traditional boundaries of casework, group work, and community work at all, but across lines, by asking ourselves what kinds of problems call for what kinds of

121

service and actions. It is possible that the ways we perceive a situation, define it, and go about treating it are shaped a priori by the particular method to which we have allegiance or in which we have skill. Perhaps—if we are bold enough to face uncertainties—treatment or intervention or planned change will defy being bound by laws or principles of governance. Perhaps knowledge and understanding plus ethics and values need only to be joined with courage, flexibility, and creative spontaneity to produce desired changes. Or perhaps, once we have genuinely and precisely described what and how we do rather than prenamed it and cast it into a method category, those detailed descriptions of new modes of action will reveal certain repeated patterns that can be put together and explained toward a generic social work theory of action.

The great federal programs for poverty prevention and for education and training call for versatile social wokers. Our present-day articulated repertoire of actions is a limited one. It needs expansion, experiment, ranging, even to risking some crazy-creative combinations that may develop and add to our ways and means of helping and changing. The characteristic of experiment as differentiated from trial and error, of course, is that underlying the former is a hypothesis, an idea about cause-effect relations, and a structured way of describing and then examining what has been done, and how and why. With this approach we will have more precise descriptions of our various practice methods. Then we can seek to articulate the practice principles they suggest.

The plea is obvious. While we give ourselves to the difficult task of developing the methods of social work we should guard against crystallizing too quickly. We should observe and describe our doing in some detail before we clap it into definition and category. We should recognize and tolerate, and even welcome, the range of differences among our several methods before we package them under generalizations that blur out those differences. Let us remind ourselves that the practice of medicine embraces both the surgeon and the psychoanalyst; teaching contains the professorial lecturer and the remedial tutor; law holds the trial lawyer and the taxation expert. Each pair is part of one profession, but they would be hard put to it to find uniformity in what they actually do. What we must recognize is that different problems and different purposes call for different interventive means and actions. Out of diversity comes richness and range; the identification of the underlying system can follow after.

Concluding Comments

It would be satisfying to be able to sum up this review of social work methods in a tidy, integrated conclusion, and to add a touch of wisdom. If ever I thought I was wise, this survey of our practice has humbled me. I am not sure I have seen straightly or clearly; I am afraid I have done no one full justice. But one impression comes clear. When in 1952 I urged that we "put the 'social' back in social work" I thought it was a lost cause. Today there is a ground swell toward this goal in every part of our practice, thrust up by passionate belief and firmed up by knowledge and reasoned appraisal. True, we are at that moment when the surge and ferment in our methods make them not yet ready for neat ordering. But their present disorder is the symptom of vigorous breakout from confining forms. It holds the potential of reorganizations and combinations of old tried and true methods and of unfenced space for experiments and innovations in action.

To the labor of examining, challenging, diversifying, assessing, and firming-up social work method our ten-year-old professional association—the National Association of Social Workers—our schools of social work, the Council on Social Work Education, and our forward-looking practitioners and agencies are all joined. The social climate has never been more invigorating. There is nothing to do but to get on with it, doggedly, and with high heart.

Self-Determination:
Reality or
Illusion?

If I were forced to answer at once the question posed by my title, instead of being given the privilege of meandering toward it, if you demanded of me, "Tell in ten words or less what your answer is," I would have to say, "I believe self-determination is nine-tenths illusion, one-tenth reality." And I would have to add, "But I believe self-determination is one of the 'grand illusions' basic to human development and human dignity and human freedom." Therefore I am committed to supporting and enhancing that illusion and also to making the most, the very most, of the exercise of that one-tenth of it that is real, present, and possible in our lives. That is what this paper is about.

Somehow, despite the fact that the concept of self-determination is old in the value system of professional social work and that it has been competently and convincingly analyzed and argued in our literature, it recurrently calls for re-examination. It seems to hold within it some conflicts and paradoxes that demand that we lift it out now and again from the matrix of our value system and view it afresh in the light of changing emphases

Social Service Review, December 1965.

and directions. We are at such a time now. Not only in social work, but in scientific and humanistic circles too, there is today an impelling interest in questions of "determinism" and freedom of the individual. We are all—social workers, clients, everyone—caught in the rising tide of a prefabricated, preplanned, preorganized, predetermined social order. We are members of a society so socialized, rationalized, organized, bureaucratized, specialized, and mechanized that there is less and less room for individual freedoms and choices. If students of our present-day life read it correctly, the problem of the individual's "other-directedness," which is to say of his responsivity to external cues and signals rather than to taking counsel with himself, and the problem of identity diffusion, which is to say of having no secure sense of self except as it is reflected back by others—these problems are endemic among us. Both are problems of some loss of selfhood. And the sense of selfhood, of humanness, of self-worth depends heavily upon the sense of self as cause. "I *am* because I *will*" is the essence of self-determination: "I am because I will to choose, to decide, to be responsible for, a cause of, the consequences that follow on my actions."

The opposing and engulfing trend in present-day life seems to make man increasingly less master of his fate. Social workers are both victims and perpetrators of this phenomenon of the planned and regularized society of this latter half of the twentieth century. Our present-day vocabulary is full of new words and phrases that bespeak new controlling trends and intents: "intervention," "reaching the hard-to-reach," "social workers as agents of change—of social control," clients or "client-systems" as "targets of change," "strategies of prevention"—and so on. Faced with what we hold to be "good" or "bad" in these trends, and with the implacable dilemmas that they present for human well-being, we struggle to hold some margin for self-affirmation by the individual. Self-determination names this margin.

It is of interest that the concept of self-determination apparently developed in social work in another decade of radical social change—in the 1930s. Before then the idea of client participation in the process of problem-solving was iterated and reiterated as both a means and an end in casework. I have not been able to discover when that subtle turn of the screw occurred that shifted "participation" with helper to "self-determination," but the newer idea was espoused by social workers with emotional intensity. Its emotional freightage is understandable when one looks at the political, economic, and psychological pressures of those times. In his critique of the principle of self-determination [1] Alan Keith-Lucas points to its relation to the liberating force of Freudian psychology. Imperative in this psychological theory was the idea that man's powers and drives needed to be freed of the inhibitions and prohibitions that shackled them. Thus casework took to the techniques of the passivity and neutrality that were characteristic of the psychoanalytic model, sometimes to points of absurdity, to be sure, but always in the hope of fostering the client's exercise of self-determination. Paralleling psychiatry was the progressive-education movement, whose interpreters and misinterpreters of John Dewey retreated from classroom controls and curriculums into permissiveness that sometimes yielded creativity in children and sometimes yielded chaos. Group work for a time took on this model.

But it was more than psychological theory that pushed social workers to make "self-determination" a professional password. The decade of the 1930s was a decade of the rise of totalitarian governments. The reaction among social workers, as among most citizens of this country, was the

---

1 "A Critique of the Principle of Client Self-Determination," *Social Work* 8 (July 1963), pp. 66—71.

passionate affirmation and reassertion of democracy and of the rights of each individual man to be his own man. Accompanying the political holocausts in Italy, Spain, and Germany was the economic holocaust in this country. What we social workers saw for the first time was that people who were or could have been our friends or relatives, who were like ourselves in background, social status, education, mores—such people in large numbers were suddenly subject to circumstances that, despite our lip-service to the contrary, we had reserved for people who were not like us. Among these circumstances were the coercions and insults and strictures that accompanied having to take relief or look for jobs or deal with creditors. Each of us thought, "There but for the grace of God go I," and each of us quaked and rebelled inwardly against the evidence that loss of economic self-dependence can mean loss of self-esteem and self-identity. So we underlined and reiterated "the client's right to self-determination" as the basic safeguard to his integrity.

Today the threats to selfhood are of a different sort—more insidious, perhaps, because they arise from social conditions and provisions that are both good and bad, provisions that eradicate one complex of social problems even as they give birth to another. These threats have been analyzed by social and political critics, often with brilliance and persuasiveness, but no powerful solutions to them have been proposed. So it seems fitting that social workers, among others who stand for humanness, should strive to hold and in some small ways to expand the narrow margin of self-determination, because it is chiefly in the exercise of his will that man knows himself and feels himself responsible for his choices and his fate.

"All theory is against the freedom of the will; all experience for it." So said the perspicacious Dr. Samuel Johnson. Now, two hundred years later, this statement still holds true. "All theory is against the freedom of the will," and all scientific and empiric fact is too. The infant organism enters the world with a constitutional set and built-in behaviors that are common to the species. It is subject from the moment breath enters the lungs to stimuli and intrusions that press in upon it physically, psychologically, socially. Each act, thought, feeling becomes linked with some experience that has preceded it, each shaped and colored by firm patterns of the culture in which the infant grows, by the patterns of the personalities with which he is in continuous transaction, and, later, by the habitual patterns which structure his own personality and behavior. Not only are physical characteristics and innate capacities predetermined, but the individual's personality, temperament, and bent are, according to recent careful longitudinal studies, fairly well set before the child has reached what can be considered to be the age of rational choice.

Yet there remains one fact to which the most rigorous of physical sciences attests: in living organisms no two cells are exactly alike; among human beings no two persons are exactly alike; and, therefore, because of the uniqueness of each man, the prediction of what he can and will do and be is not possible in any but the most general way. In other words, while each man is the product of his inheritance and his personal history, he also carries within him some part or process that breaks from the mold. It is this individuality that social workers reach for. It is this unpredictability based on each man's uniqueness, combined with the belief that as long as he is alive he is in the making, that makes room for the experience and promotion of self-determination. Dr. Johnson was right: as living is consciously experienced, we feel ourselves—or perhaps one should say the fortunate among us experience ourselves—as choosers, as deciders, as persons free to will.

We wake up in the morning trailing dreams about yesterday's or all our yesterday's problems behind our half-open eyes. We wake up not to our inner time clock, but to a clock set by a system other than our personal one. Somewhere along the way we made the choice of meeting this necessity. We get out of bed and consider what we will wear. We choose narrowly, between work-proper suits or work-proper dresses. These choices are very limited ones, because for the most part they have been made in advance by a powerful fashion and garment industry, bolstered by custom, which places role, age, and climate norms on what is or is not proper to wear. We breakfast. Will you have toast or muffins, egg or cereal, coffee black or with cream? You are not asking yourself if you will have toast or a marshmallow sundae, coffee or a gin sling, because your choices have been narrowed and limited for you by breakfast customs, by medical opinion, by parental dicta established or rebelled against long ago. But you treasure the privilege of making these small choices, limited though they are. Breakfast finished, you go to work. It is, one hopes, work you have chosen to do. How much freedom went into that choice? How far was it predetermined by conditions and people and happenstance to which you were unwittingly subject?

Yet there was some small spark or thrust in you that pushed you to want what you "chose" to do. This motive (which was itself predetermined), combined with the sense of free choice among several alternatives, is what differentiates the slave from the free man, the victim from the empowered man. If you feel that what you work at, what you do, was preordained, whether by some inexorable fate or by powers outside yourself, you will react in one of two ways. You will accept your fate with resignation and with the low level of physical and psychic energy and investment that accompanies resigned acceptance. Or, in rebellion, you will burn out those energies that might be invested in work and love. (One does not need to look far to see this proved. It is those sectors of the population whose self-determination, either as small reality or grand illusion, has been missing that are characterized by apathy and resignation or by blind impulsive revolt.) If, on the other hand, you feel that the choice of what you undertook to work at was your own choice and that, furthermore, the daily tasks involved are not so predetermined that they make you an automaton, a switch-flipper, but, rather, they allow you to exercise judgment and choice—then you feel responsible and invested in your tasks. You are "your own man."

What you choose to do, you take on as your own. Its accompanying responsibilities and rewards are acknowledged and shouldered. Even if there are frustrations involved (as must almost always happen, because there are few perfect choices in real life), even if there are disappointments or unanticipated difficulties, they are more palatable, more digestible if they are part of one's own (and owned) choice than if they were imposed from outside the self. One of the things we must learn and face about self-determination—and this is learning that desirably begins in infancy and is part of personality maturation—is that choice always involves some compromise, some renunciation. And it always involves, too, the possibility of its being a poor choice, of yielding an unhappy outcome. We take these imperfections and these chances, either by abandoning the self in a blind and helpless way to chance or fate or to dependency upon others, or by girding up our loins and taking the responsibility both for rational choices and for their consequences.

It is the thesis of this paper that self-determination, even though it may be more illusory than real, is the very essence of mature humanness; that man's exercise of choice rather than his coercion by his own blind impulses or the power of others is what builds in him his sense of effectiveness, of identity and selfhood, and of responsi-

131

bility. This is why I believe that whatever fraction of self-determination is given us should be exploited and exercised to its fullest, for ourselves and for anyone in whose lives we intervene.

In considering the social worker and the client in relation to self-determination, I have to make certain choices that contain renunciations and compromises. These choices are predetermined in part by limits of space and capacity, but in part they are "free" choices set by my judgment of what is more rather than less pertinent. I shall not touch on self-determination as it occurs in the social work methods of group work and community organization. The questions of whether the concept is equally applicable across all the social work methods or whether it is usable chiefly when the client can be designated as a "self" are worth more attention than they have had. Moreover, I shall not deal with the aspects of self-determination that have already been cogently set forth in our literature—aspects of its difference from license and impulse gratification, its inseparability from the rights of others, its dependence upon capacity for social responsibility, and so forth.[2] I shall confine myself to what the exercise of self-determination for an individual person consists of, how it fits within the framework of ego psychology, and how the social caseworker may promote and enhance it in his client.

*   *   *

2 The most relevant of these discussions, in order of their publication chronology, are: Helen Harris Perlman, "The Caseworker's Use of Collateral Information," in *Social Welfare Forum, 1951,* pp. 190–205; Anita J. Faatz, *The Nature of Choice in Casework* (Chapel Hill: University of North Carolina Press, 1953); Herbert Aptekar, *The Dynamics of Casework and Counseling* (Cambridge, Mass.: Houghton Mifflin Co., 1955); Felix P. Biestek, S. J., *The Casework Relationship* (Chicago: Loyola University Press, 1957), pp. 100–119; Helen Harris Perlman, *Social Casework: A Problem-Solving Process* (Chicago: University of Chicago Press, 1957), esp. pp. 60, 124, 132, 135; Saul Bernstein, "Self-Determination: King or Citizen in the Realm of Values?" *Social Work* 5 (January 1960), pp. 3–8; and Keith-Lucas," "A Critique of the Principle of Self-Determination," cited above.

Those persons who come into adulthood with a sense of self-respect, with a sense of being more at one with their fellow men than against them, more master of themselves and their problems than defeated, who can, in brief, be called "mature" and "adaptive"—these are persons who have had a life-experience more benign than noxious. Not everything has gone well for them. An examination of their life-histories (and we need to study many more life-histories of well-adjusted persons if we are ever going to make psychodynamic theory more than a theory of pathology) will show trauma and disappointments, mothers who fell far short of the ideal, and fathers who failed here and there. But, I would postulate, they are persons who have had a fairly continuous experience of feeling themselves to be actual or potential "cause," of being choosers and doers in contrast to being dependent upon the choices and actions of persons more powerful than they. They have had a fairly continuous and expanding experience from childhood of exercising their powers of decision and responsibility, and of having rewarding rather than hurtful consequences result from their self-determined acts.

In the development of a child the will—which is to say the assertion of drives to actualize the self—makes itself known almost at birth.[3] At birth these drives to assert self-needs and wants begin to be shaped and directed by the forces and persons with whom the infant is in continuous and expanding interaction. Every life-stage of the developing child holds innumerable daily transactions between him and others in which self-determination is

---

3 The concept "will" has in the past—and perhaps still in the present—held charged and negative connotations for many social workers, because it is central to Rankian psychology. I call attention here to its recent emergence in the writings of neo-Freudians. See in particular Erik Erikson, *Insight and Responsibility* (New York: W. W. Norton & Co., 1964), in which, among a number of references to "will" as an "ego disposition," he defines it (p. 119) as "the unbroken determination to exercise free choice as well as self-restraint."

allowed, promoted, exercised or is prohibited, restricted, blocked. There are probably some life-stages in which the assertion of the self and the developing sense of mastery are crucial. But even in the innocence of infancy the push to self-assertion can be seen. Anyone who has watched babies, even before they talk and walk, has observed the thrust and push in them to make things happen, to be the cause of consequences, to feel themselves as doers. To push toys off the high-chair tray and to find that grownups must duck and bob to pick them up is the occasion for gurgles of pleasure. Turning the face away from the proffered spoonful of mush and then the sudden grabbing of a fistful of the stuff and pushing it into the mouth—this is sheer triumph. These and like acts hold the pleasure and triumph of self-assertion.

Probably the most dramatic struggle for self-determination comes in the phase of childhood that Freud called "anal" and Erikson has described as the period when either a sense of autonomy is achieved or the child incorporates a sense of shame and doubt. In this phase the child's decision to conform to the parental will, his choices, so to speak, as to whether he will yield to training or not, and, beyond this, his coming to know both his strengths, through the exercise of all his body muscles, and his limits, through his encounter with immovable persons and objects—these experiences build into him the primitive but basic sense of self-determination which is: "I can determine—choose—whether I will hold on or give out, whether I will stay or go, whether I will yield or rebel. That power is in me. I choose to renounce some pleasures because I want the rewards, the alternate pleasurable consequences that renunciation will bring me." This is the essence of the first vital self-determination experience of the very little child. Its happy outcome depends, of course, on the combination of parental limiting and loving. Its unhappy outcome, the result of too heavy or too harsh parental domination, is seen in the child who gives up his sense of autonomy, who doubts his powers, or who, in blind revolt, becomes not self-determining at all but the victim of his own driving rage.

In the oedipal phase—or again to use the Eriksonian formulation—in the phase in which initiative or guilt is the crucial outcome, the child's experience is decisive for whether he will develop the sense that he has a selfhood of his own, separate from his parents, and that certain rights and responsibilities commensurate with his age go with this unfolding sense of self. I do not think this sense rises out of parents' permissively giving the child free choice and placing him in what is often the confusing situation of deciding whether he wants or does not want something, the nature and outcome of which he cannot even visualize. Rather it comes from parental feeding of the child's insatiable hunger to know who he is now, and where he came from, and what he is going to grow up to do and to be, and from helping him know and take pleasure in his predetermined identity. As part of this, his sense of responsibility grows as he takes into himself the qualities of those he loves and feels at one with, qualities that include the "shoulds" and the "oughts" and the "shalt nots" that begin to form the internal system of guides to what is "right" and what is "responsible."

When the child enters school his world expands and the arena for self-made decisions widens too. Simultaneously the social requirements to do and to desist from doing proliferate. He is likely to choose to go to school rather than malinger when his teacher and parents and school-mates offer him more gratification for this choice than frustration. He is likely to choose to study rather than dawdle if he finds that in his own head is the power to make sense out of those squiggles called numbers and letters. He is likely to choose to expand his horizons by moving from home into clubs and outside play if he is not coerced in one direction or another by inner fear or outer force. And he is likely to develop further his feeling of "I am," "I will," "I decide" if his activities and small hour-by-hour decisions yield results that are more rather than less gratifying. Then he achieves that resolution of the conflict of latency that Erikson called "industry versus inferiority."

Perhaps adolescence, especially in its middle and late years, presents the most unsettling and fearsome tasks of choice and decision. Decisions about what to be and what to become, choice of school, of occupation, of sexual behavior, and of sexual partner—all these and other choices are thrust upon the adolescent, plus many opportunities, plus overwhelming uncertainties, shared by parents, about what consequences may ensue. Sometimes I have thought that for the middle- and upper-class adolescent today there are both too many choices and too many possible alternatives in their world of abundance and parental permissiveness, and also too little notion of what these choices will yield in this time of moral and technological revolution. Self-determination or free choice becomes too complex and confusing when limits and boundaries are too loosely defined. Thus, we may account for the role diffusions and personal confusions pervasive among adolescents today. As for the lower-class adolescent, the world in its gaudy and glamorous representations lies open to his perceptions, exciting his wanting—but already there is for him a gaping disparity between what he will choose to have or to do and what he realistically can have or do. For him, perhaps, the problem is not role diffusion so much as role constriction; his world snaps shut too soon.

What I am trying to suggest by this whisk through child development is that by the time adulthood is reached each of us has had potent and personality-shaping experiences that determine how capable we are of grasping and using the freedoms and responsibilities of self-determination.

Such tracing through of the development or the dwarfing of the will to choose and the capacity to choose freely and realistically deserves more detailed attention. The child-parent, child-other, child-self, child-thing relationships that make up a child's world can lead to his coming to feel himself either a "doer" or a receiver of others' doing, a cause or a victim of circumstances, to experience himself as one who sees a connection between his acts and consequences or as one who defends himself against such insights, as one who has a sense of mastery or as one who feels chronically angry or depressed that he is mastered.

*   *   *

Unhappily, the clients of social workers are often persons who have not had the life-experience of continuity and support in finding and knowing themselves and in having freedoms to choose. They have been denied these freedoms. They have been smothered by others, pushed into dependency upon the powers of others; their realistic opportunities to choose among alternatives have been puny and constricted; their early assertions of self or experiments with self-chosen actions have resulted in consequences of failure or punishment, either from powerful people or from over-powering circumstances. The chronically poor, the chronically sick, the chronically outcast have rarely been self-determining. They have experienced themselves as victims and pawns, helpless except as momentary impulse or anger empowers them. Choice and self-determination have not been proffered them. So the sense of autonomy, of identity, of self as center of self-government and social responsibility—these basic images and concepts of self-hood are not often part of their personal psychology. The "right" to self-determination seems all but incredible to them, and indeed it is all but nonexistent, so narrow is the margin of their possible choices. Thus we know people as clients who have abdicated their right to choice; these are the apathetic, dependent personalities. We know clients who cling stubbornly to pseudo-autonomy by saying "No!" to people and to life; it is their only way of asserting selfhood. We know clients whose impulsive "acting-out"—which is to say their unrational drive to gratify needs—is in no sense free choice but only blind drive. Our concern must be that so many of these adults are parents of growing children whose perceptions of the world and of their being and becoming in it will be shaped and colored by their parents' interpretations and behavior.

So, for every person the social worker encounters and tries to influence, and especially for those persons who are faceless, there ought to be a conscious effort to foster, to exercise, and to enhance the choosing of actions and facing of outcomes. This exercise of self-determination may take place in any social work setting, in any single interview, and also repeatedly in the course of any case. It may be exercised in as simple and single a decision as whether or not to go to the dentist, or in as complex decisions as whether to go back to one's family or to live alone; whether to work or to follow the doctor's orders for rest; whether to try to learn to walk again or to remain in the wheelchair; whether to suffer the anger and hurt of parent-child conflicts or to suffer the guilt and hurt of self-examination toward self-change. Life-experiences for each of us are made up mostly of small decisions and only a few large ones. It is the repeated exercise of choice in these small day-to-day problems, based upon reasoned considerations of consequences and upon realistic recognition that there are few perfect solutions in life, and that, therefore, compromise and tolerance for some frustration are inherent in choice—it is this repeated exercise that builds what, in professional shorthard, we call "ego strength."

The personality operations and affects involved in self-determination are in complete congruence with the ego's functions and affects. The process, in rough outline, is like this:

The problem-to-be-solved or the question-to-be-answered must be recognized, felt by the person who faces it. Beyond awareness of it he must perceive it, see it, realistically. Perception is the primary function of the ego, basic to all functions that follow on it. Perception, to be clear and realistic, must be free of distortions created by excess need or stress and must take in both the external situation and the person's own inner responses to it.

Social workers encounter their clients in the throes of stress and crisis. In addition, their clients often do not have the knowledge by which to understand either the situation they face or their particular reaction to it. So our first job is to help the person perceive, to get the facts of, and to take knowledgeable measure of the problem in which he is involved. Simultaneously, weaving in and out of this perception of the problem, our client must be aided to see himself as reactor to and interactor with the problem, that is, as one whose feelings and responses both color the problem and affect it in ways that make it peculiarly *his* problem. The social worker's mutual and supportive exploration with his client of the nature of the problem, big or little, and the relation between it and the person's emotional involvement is the first step in enhancing the ego's perceptive functions. It is also the first step in the process of self-determination.

In the automatic operations of the ego, perception is followed or sometimes accompanied by a rallying of the mechanisms of protection or adaptation or coping. All of these may be called up at once, or in alternating sequence, or singly. For any problem that requires reasoned choice and decision the substitute for automatic process is conscious consideration. There must be lifted to the mind's eye the question of what kinds of action and reaction are possible, appropriate, useful in dealing with the problem. Between self-determination and automatic or impulsive action lies a major difference between the strong ego and the weak. The weak ego is subject to impulses or to stereotyped behavior. The adequate ego of the self-determining person has the staying power that enables the person to delay decision and action while he considers alternate modes of action, alternate possibilities, and his feelings and his capacities in relation to these possibilities.

Thus, the social worker who would help his client develop the delaying capacities that mark the difference between the primitive and the matured pleasure principle helps him to know about and to think about the possible ways in which this question or problem can be tackled. These possible ways lie in the person himself, the ways he can behave (defend himself, adapt himself to the situation, or cope with it by changing it as well as his relation to it), and they lie also in resources within and outside the social agency. Often these possible means must be introduced by the social worker. Almost always the client's thinking over, reflecting, considering the ways of acting and reacting must be stimulated, nursed, supportively coaxed along by the social worker by thought-provoking questions, tentative suggestions, supportive or provocative comments, and always the repeated underpinning of warm recognition of how hard, how tough a business it is to think something out instead of waving a wand or taking a chance.

Another major function of the ego is the anticipation of outcomes or consequences, based upon accrued and remembered past experience and/or upon new knowledge supplied by others. The strong ego carries this anticipatory function that shapes decisions. Without it the person's actions are chiefly trial and error. The anticipation of outcomes or of the possible consequences of one's choice is basic, too, to the exercise of self-determination. Free choice involves not simply deciding what one will do or have done but considering what the possible results of choice may be. In anticipating the effects or consequences of choices, the individual does two things. First, he faces up to the fact that he the chooser is in part responsible for what comes after; and, second, he recognizes that he is choosing, not between an evil and a good, not between a poor and a perfect solution, but, almost always, between better or worse, between more good and less bad, between the lesser of two imperfect outcomes. To recognize this, to chew it over, to digest it, and to "stomach it" comfortably—this is part of what we mean by ego integration. It involves the acceptance not of what I would wish for but of what I can realistically hope for, and the accompanying sense of responsibility that *I* shape my hopes and my behavior for change in the situation and/or in myself.

To enable a person to visualize and then appraise the possible consequences of his choice; to help him substitute realistic hope for childish wish; to bring him to the point at which he knows himself to be the chooser (though often a reluctant one); to help him to express, know, and handle all the new emotions that are roused by having to extend himself further to cope with difficulties ahead—to do all this takes all the technical and nurturant skills the social worker has. From this tasting, chewing, and digestion process the executive functions of the ego move out to carry into action, by overt or internal coping, the determination that has been arrived at.

It is the exercise of these functions of perception, suspended action, consideration, judgment, choice, and decision that builds into and then begins to constitute ego strength. This exercise was long ago recognized and posited as the necessary condition for the achievement of human freedom. Over one hundred years ago John Stuart Mill wrote his "Essay on Liberty," which set forth those ideas of man's freedom that have seeded all subsequent thought about self-determination. Arguing for the development of free men, Mill said: "The human faculties of perception, judgment, discriminative feeling, mental activity . . . are exercised only in making choices." He added: "The mental and moral, like the muscular powers, are improved only by being used." It is these powers and faculties that we group together in that elastic and versatile function of the personality we call "the ego," used and exercised in choice and self-determination.

One further aspect of the ego must be touched upon in this all-too-superficial review of its functions, because it bears so immediately upon self-determination. Our understanding of the ego is still very impressionistic, still very much in the unfolding. In the past two decades or so, in the shift from id psychology to ego psychology there have been some careful observations and studies that have underpinned new propositions about the nature of the ego. These propositions and their partial verifications hold promise and direction for social work. Briefly, the expanded concept of the ego is that it is far more than a messenger and mediator between inner needs and outer demands, more than defender against and neutralizer of the archaic and anarchic drives in our dark depths. It is proposed that potential ego functions come into being when the human comes into being, at birth; that the drives of the ego are autonomous, independent energies; that these drives are motored not only by conflict and frustration but by an inborn push to expand the experience of the self, the boundaries of perception, and to gain pleasure in the use of innate powers of body and mind. The ego is motivated by an "instinct to mastery." This "instinct to mastery" has been observed in young animals, babies, and young children who reach out aggressively and pleasurably to explore their small worlds at points, not of hunger and stress, but when their basic needs have been satisfied and they are in a state of "needlessness" or balance. It has been postulated, thus, that a major drive of the ego is for "effectance," which is to say for finding one's self to be the cause of an effect; and that, when that effect is gratifying, is felt to be "good," there rises in the person—child or adult—the sense of competence. To these postulates of Hartmann, Hendrick, Erikson, and White one may add the supporting conclusion that Murphy draws from her studies of young children: that "I do" precedes and is basic to the sense of "I am," [4] that the expanding sense of self follows the experience of using muscle and mind.

Look at emergent ego psychology just this far, and the relation between these ideas of the inborn push for self-actualization and the exercise of self-determination becomes apparent. The implications within any therapeutic or educative endeavor for fostering repeated practice in making responsible choices also seems clear. True, there are many things we do because we must by the currently imposed or long-ago introjected decrees of others. But our self-esteem and sense of responsibility are based upon our awareness of ourselves as cause, as mover, as chooser. Ego psychology now gives psychodynamics support to our long-held humanist philosophic stance.

If we reject self-determination as a viable means and end, if we deny its inherence in every daily transaction between ourselves and those we profess to help, then what do we choose as a workable psychology and philosophy in its place? What alternatives are there? These, in brief: A dehumanized view of man as animal or machine; a view of choice and responsibility as the right of some governing

4 Ives Hendrick, "The Discussion of the 'Instinct to Master,' " *Psychoanalytic Quarterly* 12(1943):4, pp. 561—65, and "Work and the Pleasure Principle," 12(1943): 3, pp. 311—29; Erik Erikson, *Childhood and Society* (New York: W. W. Norton & Co., 1950); Hans Hartmann, *Ego Psychology and the Problem of Adaptation* (New York: International Universities Press, 1958); Erik Erikson, "Identity and the Life Cycle," *Psychological Issues* 1:1 (New York: International Universities Press, 1959); Lois Barclay Murphy, *The Widening World of Childhood* (New York: Basic Books, 1962); and Robert W. White, "Ego and Reality in Psychoanalytic Theory," *Psychological Issues* 3:3 (New York: International Universities Press, 1963).

few—the Fascist concept, or, at its opposite pole, a state of anarchy; a view of social workers as robots manipulating other robots to the predetermined whims or plans of power-holders; a view, in short, that is intolerable to entertain.

I have come far beyond the time when I thought that if I believed in Tinker Bell she would become real. But if there is some margin of reality in a grand illusion, in an illusion that enhances the image of man, I choose to support and affirm it, to push at the boundaries of that margin to make it wider and more real. We push at that margin with every small transaction between ourselves and a client when we say to him: "What do you see as the difficulty—big or little? What do you want? What are the possible ways you can get what you want, or its reasonable facsimile? What is likely to happen one way or the other? What is bad about it? And how does that make you feel? What is good about it? Whom will it hurt or help? So, then, what is your decision, your choice? Can you stomach—or will you let me help you to stomach—the disappointments or frustrations that imperfect solutions must hold?"

Self-determination, then, is the expression of our innate drive to experience the self as cause, as master of one's self. Its practical everyday exercise builds into man's maturation process because it requires the recognition of the actual, the consideration of the possible, and, in the light of these sometime sorry prospects, the adaptation involved in decision and choice. Self-determination is based upon a realistic view of freedom. Freedom, in essence, is the inner capacity and outer opportunity to make reasoned choices among possible, socially acceptable alternatives. True, each man's exercise of self-determination is predetermined and limited by his nature and nurture, by past and present people and circumstances, and by his society's prevailing commitments to humanistic ideals. Yet within all these uniquely individual boundaries and within a larger society such as ours, which forges chains even as it speaks for liberty, within these paradoxes we must help man to find in himself some wish and power to be captain of his soul and master of his fate. We may be able to do so only in small ways. But as we support his wish and exercise his latent powers to consider and to choose, to bear compromises and to gain small pleasure from responsibly chosen outcomes—as we do this we build into each man's sense of himself as a person and affirm his worth as a human being. This one-part reality in the stubborn human illusion about self-determination is palpable and vital, ready for its potentials to be plumbed and realized.

Casework

is

Dead

Casework is dead, I repeat. Repetition is a form of self-administered brain-washing; repeat an assertion over and over again, and you come to believe it's true.

Actually I have been saying "casework is dead" with calculated aforethought for some time. Just as the declaration "God is dead" brought a high revival of interest in Him, and even defense of Him, so a rumor about the demise of casework, I have reasoned, may bring a clamor of denial. But no one has paid very much attention to me, except a few colleagues whose interests lie in other areas of social work and who give me some strongly affirming and weakly commiserating nods.

Then, a few days ago, I received a letter sent on to me by a friend who is a second-grade teacher. Her clipped-on note read, "This came in response to a form letter we send out when a kid has had a number of unexcused absences." The letter follows:

I am writing you about my daughter, Darlene. You wants to know why she stay out of school so much.

I wants you to know I works night. My hours are 4-12. I don't have the time to do what I wants to do.

Second place, I has to heat my water on the gas stove, which has 4 eyes. I has to heat the water in small pots.

Social Casework, January 1967.

I work as true, but I don't get paid until every two weeks. It is pretty tough for me. My boy friend does when ever he feels like it. I has to get cleaning out for the kids. I has to buy shoes. I think I do well for what I go through with. I am trying to move also.

I wish you or somebody would come to the homes of kids that don't come to school like you wants them to, and see just what happen.

When kids Darlene's age stay out of school, its a reason, and a good reason to. You don't know what people go through with in they home.

I want you to know I don't get no aid of any kind. I got news for you. I don't want any aid. I got my health and strength.

So I hope you understand just what I am talking about. Darlene can always go to summer school and catch up.

Mrs. Louella May Jones.[1]

Following my long-entrenched caseworker's habit, I read the letter a second time to catch what lay between the lines.

". . . I works night. My hours are 4-12." That means waiting in the dark for those slow-coming, lonely buses. Walking down the black, menacing street. One o'clock or later to bed. Meaning to get up on time—but when the morning stir of the children breaks through her sleep—oh, the lethal drowsiness, the burrowing down in for one more moment of oblivion. So Darlene's being roused and dressed and breakfasted and sent off to school becomes a sometime thing. . . .

"I has to heat the water in small pots." No swivel of a faucet for a rush of hot water to wash up hands and faces, to rinse out the small, greying underpants or the soiled socks. (Why must kids find the dirtiest stoops to sit on, the wettest gutters to wade across?) Wait for the water to heat in that skimpy-sized pot, dip your fingers, dab your nose, heat up some more; begin again on that pile of yesterday's

---

1 You are, of course, free to decide for yourself about the truth or fiction of this whole account. The letter, however, is a verbatim copy of an actual one, with only the names changed. I owe it to Constance Sherrard.

clothes—with time running out, irritation running high.

"My boy friend does when ever he feels like it." A woman needs a boy friend. A woman with kids needs a husband—someone, that means, to conserve her, to gather her to him with all her faults and troubles and warm her, to care for her and the family they have together. But if she has no husband, she needs a boy friend, to keep her company, and tease and fool around for laughs, to make her feel warm and alive in the dark. But he doesn't have to do for her unless he feels like it. So she wheedles or pleads or threatens; or the children—they're not his kids maybe, but they're *kids* just the same—by their need of him, pull at his compassion. *Maybe,* she thinks, he'll marry me some day. *Maybe*—if he can get a steady job and some chesty chick with no kids doesn't grab him first.

"I wish you or somebody would come to the homes of kids that don't come to school like you wants them to, and see just what happen." Could *you* do it? Could *you* cope—morning after too-short night? Waking in that cold-water flat, slum-filthy, so that washing and cleaning is for nothing; the kids racketing and scrapping for the crumbs of last night's sweet rolls or crumbs of mamma's notice and attention, hanging hungrily on her skirts or searching her closed face with round, anxious eyes. Is there milk for breakfast—or did the groceryman say, "No more credit"? Is there bread—or did that Darlene forget to stop for it? Is the littlest one crying because he's just ornery—or sick? Has he been picking at that broken plaster again? Is there time to hustle him off to the clinic and wait for the doctor—or to go call the landlord (if a dime's around) to tell him he's got to close up those rat holes? And get some supper worked up and some ironing done, and go see if the shoemaker can fix that broken heel, and be ready to catch that three o'clock bus? "...it's a reason, and a good reason to. You don't know what people go through with in they home."

"I got news for you. I don't want any aid. I got my health and strength." Spunky woman she is, full of—what is it? Pride? Self-respect? Anger? Distrust of that organized, efficient office world of papers and forms and questions that ask "How much?"—Where is the children's father?"—"Who is your boy friend?"—"Why don't you work?" or, perversely, "Why *do* you?" Isn't fierce independence always mixed with smoldering hostility? And does that anger and unrelenting self-demand spill over onto Darlene and the younger children? Does she give them no quarter because she's had none? What does it cost her, I wonder, this bitter pride of self-sufficiency?

"Darlene can always go to summer school and catch up." Darlene has a whole lot of time ahead of her, she must feel, and school's always there. That's how it is for poor folks: mostly you've got to do with how you can. It's true. Darlene has time. She's seven or so now—probably already behind in her reading and numbers because she's been absent so much. And when she's there, she's only half-awake; or she's quaking inside because she came late again and the teacher looks at her as if she's bad; or she's sitting stony-faced in that crowded black-boarded room crying inside because mama yelled and said she is going to give her and the whole bunch away if things don't get some better. She has time, all right—to grow afraid of school, to barricade her mind against it; finally to be walled off from it. By the way, Mrs. Jones, did you know—there is no summer school for dropouts from the second grade.

I got up from Mrs. Jones's soiled sagging chair—figuratively, you understand—and sat down with determination at my desk. Darlene and her mother, I reminded myself firmly, are only a single instance of widespread, endemic social problems. I pushed the family from the center of my mind and mobilized myself to think of ways and means—strategies, I think the word is—by which such problems could be eradicated, at best, or ameliorated, at least. What is needed, I told myself, is social planning on a significant scale, basic preventive intervention, with macro-systems—*system*-change not simply *symptom*-change. What all the Darlenes and Mrs. Joneses need are such human welfare programs and social policies as will expand the narrow margins of their lives and undergird their precarious existence. So I drew up a list of specific needs that such a program should meet:

1. Need for decent housing: accelerated slum clearance; building of adequate, low-cost, integrated, small-unit homes

2. Need for economic security: a guaranteed minimum income or some kind of family allowance that will maintain a flow of economic security at the same time that incentives to work (for money or for self-realization) are provided

3. Need for the nurture of children (affectional and social as well as physical): nurseries, day care programs for use by either working or nonworking mothers; classes or discussion groups of mothers to give attention to their needs and frustrations and to teach them about what children need and are like and what mothering involves ("indigenous" personnel, under professional guidance, in these programs); in addition, homemaker programs, both for home care of children when necessary and household-management guidance

4. Need for freely and quickly accessible medical aids, especially pregnancy prevention—or pregnancy protection

5. Need for community service centers: available personnel to pick up the small, loose-end, crucial problems as well as to co-ordinate services and guide people to established resources and opportunities (nonprofessional helpers in these centers, trained and guided by collaborating teams of doctors, social workers, nurses, school representatives, and clergymen); parent and marital coun-

seling discussion groups to offer company and socialization, not just information; job training; recreation referrals; and so on and so on.

And so on, and so on—the possibilities burgeoned and began to run away with me. The basic need, I saw, was for social planners and social actionists who could think big, see far, plan with creativity and sagacity.

So I took my few rough notes and Mrs. Jones's letter to one of my colleagues who, in my opinion, has these capacities, and who has been very nice to me in spite of my being a caseworker.

He read the letter soberly. "What are you going to do?" he asked. I showed him my prospectus.

"But my good woman," he said, "this situation won't sit around waiting for all this to get going!"

"I know," I said humbly, "but I feel it's necessary to get to the heart of the matter."

"By the time you get to the heart," he said severely, "Mrs. Jones's heart will be eaten out and Darlene will have started a new generation."

"True," I mused, "but—"

"No *but's* about it," my friend said, raising his voice. "You ought to get this into the hands of a good social agency at once!"

"But how so?" I cried. "Isn't it pretty extravagant to pour expensive time and energy and community money into one little Darlene and her mother when thousands of families need the same kind of help?"

"If you were a doctor," my friend asked patiently, "would you pass by the man sick with malaria because you were trying to track down the anopheles mosquito?"

I had to admit I would not, or that I would, at least, call in a colleague to do one task while I did the other. "Just the same," I added, "how can we prove that a social worker would help Darlene and Mrs. Jones? What research is there on outcomes," I protested, "that shows conclusively that intervention in a single case on a one-to-one basis will be successful?"

My friend tended to his pipe. "You are naive," he said to me in his finest nonjudgmental tone. "Is education—at any level—'successful'? Is religion 'successful'? Moreover, is the man you just successfully cured of malaria not likely to have chills and fever again unless provision is made to buttress your medicine?"

"There's another thing," my friend said, rising as if to give a lecture. "That is that even if we had available all the welfare opportunities you've dreamed up, Mrs. Jones might just not want to use them. She might just not be willing to give up that 4-12 work shift. She might just not be interested in anything beyond herself and her boy friend. She might just need someone to help her see things differently and feel things differently in order to want what we happen to think is good for her and the kids. And moreover," he said—there was no stopping him now—"read your history and examine the phenomena of social change and progress. Each utopia breeds its own special human needs."

"But that means," I said, shaken now, "that you'll need *caseworkers*—or whatever you'd call them—to attend to people one by one, to try to ease their small personal miseries, to influence how they see and feel about themselves and their lives so they can act in different and more satisfying ways."

"Call them what you will," said my friend with some asperity. "But there will always be individuals who can't or who won't, who want but can't get, who reach but can't grasp, who want more or better or different."

"But," I whispered, "I thought casework was dead."

"You and your Freudian death wishes!" he snorted. "For heaven's sake, get someone out to visit Mrs. Jones—she's asking for it—get someone who'll give her full credit for all her get-up-and-go and her gumption and who'll understand her aches and her angers. And someone who'll help her to want her kids to have the opportunities that are open and ready for them right now. That's all I'm saying!"

I felt chastened and said I would. But first I got him to promise that he, on his part, would continue to work on the plans for social provision and prevention and system changes and all that sort of thing.

Can
Casework
Work?

In the past five years or so casework has become the whipping boy of social work. A whipping boy, it will be remembered, was usually a promising young lad brought up as the alter ego of a promising young prince. He represented, in a socially structured way, the "badness" of the prince, and he was punished for the prince's misdeeds or delinquencies. This practice enabled the parents and critics of the prince to get a lot off their chests and onto the whipping boy's backside, and thus it had considerable therapeutic value for them. It also enabled the prince to develop his sense of self-esteem and self-regard and general omnipotence and thus had considerable therapeutic value for him. There are no records of what it did to the scapegoat himself—but it is conceivable that the scoldings and beatings may have had some therapeutic value for him too. It would have been too bad if he had actually incorporated all the blame directed at him and settled for beating his breast and crying "Mea culpa." But it might have been less bad—maybe even growth-producing—if he had taken a good hard look at his

Social Service Review, December 1968. This is drawn in part from the author's chapter in *The Multi-Problem Dilemma,* "Casework and the Case of Chemung County"(53).

role, recognized it as being socially, not personally, designed, and then identified the difference between what he actually had done and what he was being whipped for.

Caseworkers, it has seemed to me, have had several differing reactions to their current whipping-boy status. Some have withdrawn into cool isolation; some have confessed to everything, sins of mission, omission, commission; some have identified with the aggressors and have cried out against caseworkers, not themselves but all those other caseworkers who are to blame, all those others who ought to be in there where the action is, doing everything from organizing the indigenous to washing up his children and trotting them off to school. There are, however, other caseworkers—and I am only one among them—who are trying to take a good hard look at what casework really is, what its social design and purpose can be expected to be, and whether the energy that is going into self-recrimination and other-recrimination can be directed and released into better social service.

The boundaries of a single paper make it impossible to deal with some of the preliminary and basic questions about where in the total social system social work belongs and how social work as a profession can operate more effectively in the over-all purpose of social welfare. Here I propose to deal only with one process of social work—casework. I propose to speak for that whipping boy who looks up from his welts and asks: "What am I?" "What am I for?" and "Can I justify or even have respect for my role?"

That those of us who are caseworkers must stop and make this hard, cool assessment is, I submit, essential to our self-respect and our sense of social purpose. But more than this: it is essential to decisions about whether or not casework has value at all, and for whom and under what conditions. These latter considerations become imperious not simply because we are under the fire of criticism but also because we are increasingly under the careful and objectively designed scrutiny of research that is asking. "What is the outcome of your input? What exactly do you make happen by your treatment efforts?"

Has Casework Failed?

It will be remembered that the much quoted study, *Girls of Vocational High,*[1] revealed only small and statistically nonsignificant differences between the girls who had had "casework treatment" and those who had not, insofar as their problematic behaviors and attitudes were concerned. These findings were given considerable play not only within social work but in the public press; they "proved" people's dark suspicions about the futility of social work. Only a few months ago there appeared in print another book that presents another study of casework efforts.[2] It shows that between cases on public assistance carried by unselected relief investigators and those carried by two caseworkers with Master's degrees there was no significant difference in progress or outcomes. As all the cases in this study were identified as "multiproblem families," both professional and subprofessional workers had like complexities facing them. The help of the two trained caseworkers was to be "family-centered." Beyond this, the difference lay in the fact that the two trained caseworkers had the alleged advantage of social work education and, moreover, had caseloads carefully limited in number, while the regular workers carried their usual heavy loads. Like *Girls at Vocational High,* this study has shown that

---

1 Henry J. Meyer, Edgar F. Borgatta, and Wyatt C. Jones, *Girls at Vocational High: An Experiment in Social Work Intervention* (New York: Russell Sage Foundation, 1965). For a trenchant analysis of this research, with particular relevance to the unrealistic casework means and expectations utilized, see Mary E. Macdonald, "Reunion at Vocational High," *Social Service Review* 40 (June 1966), pp. 175–89. See also Correspondence section, *Social Service Review* 40 (September 1966), pp. 320–23.
2 *The Multi-Problem Dilemma* (Metuchen, N. J.: Scarecrow Press, 1968).

casework rode again and fell off its high horse. Or at least it has shown that two trained caseworkers fell off, and I am concerned that these findings will be used to "prove" that casework does not work.

Whatever the merits (or faults) of the two studies, I find one thing wrong with them. It is the same thing that is wrong with a great many discussions, whether defenses of or diatribes against casework. It is that the concept of casework, of what it is and under what conditions it can operate, is not at all carefully or precisely defined. It is exactly here that caseworkers, not researchers, are to blame. We are to blame, not because we have not righted all social wrongs, but simply and massively that we have not clarified even for ourselves what casework is, what its particular limits and its particular possibilities are. Not having clarified this for ourselves, we have not clarified it for those researchers or the public man who would assess our efforts.

We are to blame, not because we have not been able to keep girls from becoming pregnant out of wedlock, not because we have not been able to transform lethargy into avidity, not because we have not been able to make the chronically poor become sturdily middle-class. We are to blame because we have implicitly promised that we could and would. We are to blame because we have oversold our powers and our purposes, not in any malicious intent to mislead either the public or the researcher, but in some naive megalomania of which we ourselves have been victims. We have said, "If we had more caseworkers . . . if we had lower caseloads . . . if we had more time"—as if quantitative lacks were all that stood in the way of our effectiveness. Even today schools of social work and federal agencies and state legislatures talk about the manpower problem in social work as if it were indeed only a matter of lack of persons to fill the open jobs. I submit that the manpower problem needs to be viewed as a *mind-power* problem, a problem of reappraising and redesigning the kinds and modes of services that ought to be available to people who need supports or aids to more gratifying and competent daily living. Casework will be one of those modes, I believe, but only one, and not necessarily the major one. The point here is that if we are to answer the question, "Does casework work?" we must add "Under what conditions?" "Related to what powers in the client?" "For what kinds of problems?" "Toward what realistic goals?"

What is Casework?

Casework is one process in social work. It is only that: one process. The other major processes by which social work carries its purposes into action are group work and community work. To rule out some common misinterpretations, it should be reiterated that casework is not a bundle of services that can be "delivered," as present parlance has it, to those who "need it." It is not a social program. Indeed, it is a misnomer to call an agency "a casework agency," as if this process is what the agency "gives." An agency should be named by its purpose—child welfare or family service. It should be named by the social problems it proposes to deal with. It may, then, use casework as one of its processes. It may also use other processes of influence—work with groups, with organizations, and so on. This is not merely a semantic play. It deserves—but cannot have here—careful consideration because if a program is named by one process it is constricted. If it is named by the problem it endeavors to deal with, then a range of processes may be incorporated.

The process called casework holds many likenesses to the two other major processes of social work. Its values and human welfare commitments are the same; so are many of its guiding principles of action. It is different largely because of its focus. Casework focuses upon the "case," the single, individual unit in society, whether that unit is one person or a family. Its focus is upon the small but vital arena in which social-psychological problems are encountered by the living human being, are felt, struggled with, sweated out, wept or bled over, and are capitulated to or overcome.

The problems with which casework helps the individual (or family) to cope are multiple-diverse problems in interpersonal transactions—between one person and another or between himself and social circumstances. The person's or family's difficulty in coping successfully is assumed to be related to one or to a combination of the following lacks: lack of motivation to cope, lack of capacity to cope, or lack of the resources and opportunities.[3] Thus the process of casework attempts to engage and influence the resources within both agency and community so that they become usable, and those within the particular clients themselves toward heightening the possibility that they may satisfactorily and gratifyingly carry their everyday love and work tasks.

That is all. That "all" involves deep and swift knowledge of the inner workings of people, and of their interpersonal operations, much skill in relationship and empathy, and other modes of influence that cannot be delineated here. Whatever knowledge and skill the caseworker possesses, there must be at base a realistic appraisal of the persons to be helped, what they want and what they expect, what they can be expected to be and to do, what their particular problems are and how they are experienced, how amenable these problems are to present skills of treatment, and what

---

3 For elaboration of these ideas see Helen Harris Perlman, *Social Casework: A Problem-Solving Process* (Chicago: University of Chicago Press, 1957), esp. pp. 54–57, 183–203; and Lilian Ripple, *Motivation, Capacity, and Opportunity: Studies in Casework Theory and Practice,* "Social Service Monographs," 2d ser., no. 3 (Chicago: School of Social Service Administration, University of Chicago, 1964), pp. 19–52.

resources are available for use in the social environment. Only a realistic appraisal of this complex of factors will produce a realistic design for what the caseworker's input should be and what the expectable outcome can be. One can be a Mesmer, a Freud, a Mary Richmond all combined, yet, unless the forces within the person and his present social situation are assessed and appropriate goals are set, there is likely to be failure.

This defining of casework, and the delineation of the specific and realistic conditions and expectations and goals based upon the specific population under study, did not occur in the two studies I have cited. Herein was laid the groundwork for the unhappy findings. For this caseworkers, not researchers, must be primarily responsible.

The illustrations that follow are presented not because they are "horrible examples" but rather because they are commonplace examples of the way we caseworkers set our own traps.

The families chosen for the experiment recorded in *The Multi-Problem Dilemma* were designated as "multiproblem families." What does this designation mean?

"Multiproblem family" is not a diagnosis. It has no specificity or classifying value. It says only that family has many problems. But anyone knows that problems have chain reactions and that a problem of money-deficit is likely to affect health, and the presence of these two deficits is likely to create a sense of stress, and so on. "Multiproblem" as it is used today often embraces such diverse categories as "lower-class," "chronically poor," "socially disorganized," "noncommunicative," "hard-to-reach," "hard-core." What do we mean? The caseworker must ask and answer this question. If we are to plan intervention with a group of "multiproblem" families we must identify clearly what kinds of problems characterize them and make it valid to consider them a homogeneous group. Then, having gone only so far, the next step before

161

taking action needs to be the selection of what problems would be focused upon. What are the priority problems? the targets? For some problems there are services to be had, for others there are not. For some we have skills; for others we do not. Which would be the problems in focus, the problems to be worked? Only with some answer to this question can caseworkers plan what to do and what some achievable goals may be.

And what does "family-centered treatment" mean? Reading across casework writings on the subject of family-centered treatment, one is aware of many meanings: The caseworker's over-all concern is for the welfare of the whole family; the family is the unit for the interview; the family is the unit of concern, but one key member is the selected (self- or worker-selected) problem-solver; the family is the unit of concern, and interviews may be held with one member or all or several. And these meanings create considerable difference when they are translated into action. The family as a working unit, for example, requires time and place arrangements quite different from those required for a one-member interview. Moreover, it requires of the caseworker skills in group and relationship management that are only now being identified. Further, it makes research on who improves as reported by whom a rather tricky proposition.

What are the Worker's Multiple Problems?

Multiple problems multiply problems, not only for the client but for the caseworker too. One of the common reasons for a person's inability to cope with multiple problems is that he feels overwhelmed by their complexity. He must do one of several things, in accordance with the laws of human behavior under stress: he retreats from the situation, into apathy or sickness or denial; he tries to tackle it, but because he feels overwhelmed he tends to do so in ways that are more disorganizing than problem-solving. Multiple problems flood their carriers with a sense of futility and helplessness and excite in them either feelings of defeat and hopelessness or anxiety so high that it leads to poorly planned, poorly aimed, disintegrated activities. This, in crude outline, is the basic explanation for the futile behavior and poor adaptation that are so frequently seen in those families who live under chronic stress.

What has perhaps not been given adequate recognition is that caseworkers also operate according to laws of human behavior under stress. Caseworkers also may find themselves flooded and overwhelmed by the burgeoning of problems that pop out from all directions as soon as they give an attentive eye and ear to a family situation or a gentle probe to a "presenting" problem. Caseworkers, too, then, may be caught up in a number of defensive maneuvers in the effort to reinstate their balance: they may retreat from the overwhelming situation by writing it off as "hopeless"; they may retreat into the protection of "professional magic" by going through certain rituals of words and actions; or—and this is probably the most frequent—they may hold their ground and take on everything they see or that comes at them, indiscriminately, in a scattered and disorganized (and further disorganizing) way, with all ten fingers plugging holes in the dike, so to speak, and leaks springing out all about.

Turn now to look at the problems that were probably faced by the two trained caseworkers who set out to "do casework" with a caseload of multi-problem public assistance clients. The probability is that, with a limited number of cases and with frequent visits to their clients, the trained caseworkers were far more aware of the number and complexities of the problems in their families than the usual public assistance worker would be. The latter would visit infrequently, on a touch-and-go basis, with a clear charge to focus upon need and eligibility. Scratch the surface of any family and you will find conflicts and problems—they are inherent in human beings' living together. When "the problem" is defined by both investigator and client chiefly as money-need and its provision is arranged with adequacy and regularity, other problems may fade into the background. When the problem is defined as "multiple," and the charge is to be "family-centered," the caseworker opens a Pandora's box. Everything flies up at once. Greater awareness with its inevitable attendant anxiety is more likely for the professionally prepared caseworker than for the person who is not so alerted. As a result of education in diagnostic thinking, the trained worker may not only recognize more problems but may attribute greater significance to them than would a less clinically oriented worker.

This is not to say that the diagnostically trained caseworker is always correct in his appraisal, and certainly it is not to say that his insights are always relevant. Often they are not.[4] The result may be that the trained worker becomes paralyzed by seeing too much.

This very sensitized perception may serve to swamp him unless he has some firm footing provided by some predetermined understanding about what his treatment focus is to be and what the reasonable expectations are. While the regular public assistance caseworker is, indeed, regularly "swamped," he is swamped by work volume and procedural detail too great to be encompassed in the limits of work time. But he has the advantage of a clearly delimited purpose and service: the provision of basic economic and health needs. The trained caseworker, on the other hand, charged with the ambiguous task of dealing with all the problems he discerns in a caseload of

---

4 This is a problem, it must honestly be said, that casework courses in many schools of social work have not yet mastered: that their focus on elaborations of diagnosis far outstrips and outweights their focus upon its utility for treatment.

multiproblem, multipeopled families may find himself in a situation in which he sees and knows too much about too many things over which he has too little control (or for which no reparative resources as yet exist). Moreover, he finds himself under some expectation because he is "professional" that what he will do will in some way be more elegant than run-of-the-mill. When this expectation is vague and unidentified, it can only add to the already distracting and disorganizing setup he enters.

Turn now to the client. Paramount in the determination of what he will or will not do is his own wishing and wanting and willing—his motivation for change. Motivation is a many-layered thing. What I refer to here are those conscious or close-to-the-surface feelings and ideas about what one needs and wants, and about how much it is worth stretching for. Can we simply assume that the client who takes money assistance wants or feels the need for the other forms of aid and service that an agency decides he needs and ought to want? Like all the rest of us, the person with multiple problems is both driven and strait-jacketed by a complex of motivations. In differing degrees these combine realistic hope and far-fetched wish, aspiration and resignation, wanting yet fearing. The client's motivations, like any other person's are further determined by the values of his particular reference group, values about what is good and what is bad, what is necessary and what is disposable, what is crucial and what can wait. Does he want "rehabilitation"—whatever that is—just because he needs money?

The point is that one cannot set forth to "do intensive casework" or proffer service for persons with multiple problems with the jaunty confidence of a salesman carrying a case full of bright gadgets for every household need. One cannot help wonder what those clients chosen for "intensive casework" thought when they found themselves the subject of weekly rather than half-yearly visits, of eager inquiries and offers rather than the long-accustomed remoteness of the agency. Perhaps we social workers are so buoyant with our own intentions that we do not stop to consider how those intentions are read and interpreted by those we would help.[5]

The beginning and repeated question is "What does the client want—what is his sense of need and urgency and reachable goal?" Even such simple things as learning to put a room in order or keeping a clinic appointment or getting up in time to send the children to school—even these simple acts may take considerable effort and conscious reorganization of a client's habitual behavior. So they will take some inner push in the client himself to do them. This is why the caseworker must first and always attune himself to what his client is driving toward, and especially is this the case when the agency and not the client decides a change is in order.

Another aspect of the casework process needs touching on. In the past few years there has been a flood of light cast upon the "culture" of the poor, of the educationally as well as economically disadvantaged. Certain kinds of behavior, of cognitive modes, of attitudes, of self-other concepts and relationships tend, it is held, to characterize the majority of persons who make up the membership of the long-and-poorest poor. Certainly every individual in this class-culture will not conform to this characteristic pattern, any more than every middle-class individual is a walking incarnation of his class. With this warning against the substitution, one needs to examine the findings of the numerous studies that bear on the ways the lower-class, chronically disadvantaged person feels and acts.

Every "typical" characteristic of behavior or attitude

---

5 This, parenthetically, is not limited to social workers who are caseworkers. Today's "social actionists" are guilty of this same assumption: that, because their angers burn at social injustice and because they are driven to right those wrongs, the victims of injustices must surely welcome both them and their schemes.

among any group of persons should have some implication for the way a caseworker will act. It should design both what he will do and how he will do it. The characteristics of the men, women, and children who are the victims-creators of the "culture of poverty" must serve case-workers not as pejorative labels for disposal purposes but rather as guides to the means and modes of intervention.

The fact is that casework's articulated body of principles of conduct and influence stems from a predominantly middle-class psychology and a middle-class value system.[6] This is not a pejorative statement either. It is a fact that has action implications. A whole series of "if-then" propositions governs what and how the case-worker must act. The "if" says, "If this person adheres to a certain value system, he will tend to think-act-feel in certain ways"; "then," we say, "one anticipates and says and acts in certain congruent ways if one is to influence him." What the newly emergent findings on the culture of the poor suggest is the necessity for a revised set of "if-then" propositions. If it is true, for example, that the long-poor tend to be more present-oriented than future-oriented, then today's problem will have to be in the center of the worker's and client's attention. If there is little capacity among this group to postpone gratification and a strong tendency to be impulse-ridden, then rewards for efforts made and the meeting of pressing needs must come at once and be frequent. If members of this group tend to be concrete-minded, unaccustomed and therefore unable to deal with abstract notions, if they most truly know what their sensory organs tell them is there, then casework communication must be plain and simple and the aids offered must be those that can be seen and felt. If there is little experience in this group of the luxury of introspection—for it is a luxury, available only to those who do not continuously have to scan the outside dangers

---

6 So does that of group work and of community work. Indeed, the concept of "maximum possible participation" is a middle-class concept.

in their lives—if these persons have not experienced the benefits of lifting feeling to the mind for its consideration, then the caseworker must know that talking, even for ventilation, will be held of small use, and that only action (on the client's part or on that of the worker), action that brings quick results, must be counted on to change feelings rather than the other way around.

In short, it is possible that contributing to casework failure in treatment has been the maintenance of treatment modes that have not been appropriate to the motivations and capacities of certain client groups. If this is true, then we ought to leave off with both breast-beating and evaluative research for a time and work instead on new adaptations of our problem-solving process.

What are the Conditions for Effective Casework?

Assuming that we have made the necessary and desirable changes and shifts in the casework process—that we have become more clear about what casework is and is not, more focused and modest about what we undertake, more precise about identifying the problems with which we can deal, more realistic about possible goals, more attuned to the differences in motivations and meanings among the several class and ethnic groups—an insistent question remains. It is the question of the use of casework in situations in which basic economic needs, basic social supports, basic psychological security are and have been pervasively and persistently absent. Since casework is chiefly a process by which to promote and enhance people's ability to function with gratification and competence, and not a panacea or a laying on of healing hands or a giving out of magical aids, must there not be present certain conditions of psychological and social and economic resource in order for this process to work? Or, to turn the question about, are there psychological and socioeconomic conditions that make casework help minimally effective?

Present-day ego psychology may serve as a partial reference frame here. One of its major theoreticians[7] proposes that human beings are driven by two major kinds of needs: one, to fill in "deficit needs," that is, to gratify basic biological and psychosocial wants; and, second, to fulfill "developmental needs," that is, to gratify strivings for growth, competence, self-actualization. "Deficit needs" include such physical wants as hunger and sex but also include the more distinctly human need for love and affection, for a dependable "floor" of economic and social security, and, beyond this, for a sense of having some recognizable place and function in a social system. When these deficit needs have been met (or can be hoped for with confidence), and only then, is the individual free to turn his energies outward to striving to be and to have more or better than he is and has. Only then is he free to take the risks involved in changed ways of behaving; only then is he free to invest himself in other persons, or interests, or tasks. In short, a person's ability to reach out, to strive, change, adapt, reshape behavior and attitudes, to invest himself in new tasks—all these capacities and strivings depend upon his having had enough security of an economic, physical, affectional, and social sort in the past that he can bank on, or enough in his present that he feels himself to be relatively on solid ground and in balance. Then he is ready to look ahead and beyond with some confidence.

Reverse the picture. If income has been chronically inadequate to meet basic food, shelter, clothing, and personal-incidental needs; if tensions ride long and high within the person because of his chronic frustration and, thus, inevitably affect his capacity to relate with trust and

---

7 A. H. Maslow, *Motivation and Personality* (New York: Harper & Row, 1954).

loving to other people; if, added to this chronic experience of feeling want and being found wanting, he feels social denigration and constriction; if there is and has been closure of social opportunity for adequate role performance and consequent social recognition, then a person is caught in a multiproblem trap. His life-energies will be eaten up by rage or depression or by his dull drudging to manage or make do at a minimal level, with no energy surplus for new approaches to his problem. Depletion of energy—as anyone who has ever been only physically exhausted knows—results in depletion of incentive, effort, striving.

Now the caseworker comes in. If the need is for money for food, housing, clothing—and if the caseworker can furnish the money—then he can meet one basic deficit need. If, however, there is no money to be had or allowed, then the caseworker, by his sympathy and appreciative understanding of his client's rage or desperation, can help him only to endure this deficit. He or his kindly ministrations cannot take the place of money deficits.

If this immutable deficit need is compounded by ill-health or physical disability in one or more family members, and if the caseworker can find medical aids and, in addition, can help the client use them, then he may start some change going. But the medical resources must be there. Morever, physical malfunctioning (like many kinds of social and psychological malfunctioning) may take its inexorable course despite the best of medical care. So while the effort has been made no actual change may occur. This deficit will not have been filled in.

If physical disability combines with family conflict or family disorganization, then the caseworker may offer the opportunity to talk over, think over, feel over these problems so that family life may meet its major function: to fulfil the basic protective and affectional needs of its members. Indeed, one of the deficits that contact with an empathic caseworker frequently helps to meet is this one of affectional hunger. Working always to create and sustain a relationship that is concerned and compassionate, the caseworker often provides some substitute experience of being liked or cared for, respected too, to persons whose hunger for affection and recognition is rarely met in their everyday lives. But a casework relationship cannot be a permanent substitute for that which must be found and sustained in the client's own family and friendship groups. So affectional deficits may be only partly met.

Talking over, thinking over, feeling over one's problems of person-to-person or self-to-situation relationships requires some freedom from other stresses. The examination of one's own behavior, the introspective exploration of the self as "actor" and "feeler" and "thinker" is, as has been said, a luxury usually available only to those who are free to take their eyes off the manifest dangers outside. Moreover, it requires some co-operation from the "others" involved in the problem. Beyond this, it requires some capacity to express things in words, to trust in the efficacy of talk, some experience of thinking as a rewarded delay of or substitute for action. All these capacities are often hard to find in the culture and habitual conduct of multi-problem, "hard-to-reach" families.

The third type of basic need is that of having some secure niche in a social system and some recognized and accredited function there. It is the need for a respectable social role that one can carry with a relative sense of adequacy and social affirmation. In any society, to be an "in" one must be able to carry certain tasks in certain expected ways: a husband is expected to be a breadwinner; a woman with children is expected to meet the nurture needs of her children, both physical and affectional; an adolescent is expected to be a student on his way to some occupational role—and so on. The needs that are met by these activities are those of social recognition and anchorage and the combined rewards of social approval and self-esteem that accrue to their being well done.

One of the major deterrents to recognized adequacy in social functioning is the actual lack of means by which to carry a role. This "lack of means" may lie in the person himself—in mental, physical, or emotional handicaps. But it may also lie in life-conditions of the person, in his family, or the community. If a job is not to be had, a man cannot be a breadwinner. If day care for children is not to be had, a mother cannot go out to learn work skills. If soap and mops and dresser drawers and closets are not to be had, a woman cannot be a good housekeeper. If homemaker service is not to be had, if decent housing is not to be had, if special classes for retarded children are not to be had, then these deficits in social provisions will have their deficit consequences in individual social functioning. No casework process can substitute for them.

Traditionally, the caseworker has served to firm up and weave the lines of connections between individuals and organized social provisions. Traditionally, he works both sides of the transaction—to facilitate the client's knowledge of the resource and to influence him to use it, and to prepare the resource to lend itself to the applicant in the light of his special needs. These arrangements and ongoing linkages and supports are vital ways by which caseworkers find and fill in social deficit needs, but the resources must be present. A caseworker cannot manufacture them on the spot. He can, and does, and should repeatedly point to and decry their absence when they are lacking and interpret the need for them to his own agency, to his professional organization, and to other welfare-minded groups in the community. Out of these deficit needs identified by caseworkers over the years have grown the many kinds of useful social services that exist today. Until they are present, however, the caseworker and today's "multi-problem family" may be blocked for want of social resources.

Perhaps what is called the "multiproblem" family would be better identified as a "multideficit" family. The caseworker encounters in it not one but a complex of deficit needs. And it is probable that an inverse relationship exists between chronic and pervasive needfulness and the capacity to "move," "change," "adapt," "improve." Until physical, affectional, and social hungers have had some fulfillment (one will not say "been satisfied," for that would be unrealistic), until a floor of security is felt as certain, people are not free to look or reach beyond the here and now. "More and better" are hoped for and striven for only when minimal needs have been met and felt as secure somewhere within the life-cycle. Relationships with other people may be improved only when the energy that is being used to lick one's own body and soul wounds can be released outward from the self. The need for love (or its reasonable facsimile) must have been fed before there grows the reciprocal capacity to "give out" with love or to invest one's self in other people or social responsibility. Taking the responsibilities and gaining the rewards that participation in social involvements afford—church or school or voluntary groups—begins with the will and energy to "put one's self out," and this, in turn, depends on the confidence that one's efforts will be gratifying rather than futile. The motivation for change, for the more constructive use of one's self, is dependent on some surplus of free energy; on some confidence accrued over the years that things can be bettered by personal effort; and on the presence of tangible, touchable, reachable means.

The casework process does not and cannot substitute for basic deficit needs, and it ought not to be assessed nor its results measured as if it could. It is dependent upon certain other life-conditions being present and viable. Just as an orthopedist could scarcely teach his patient to walk again without the sticks and braces and other rehabilitative devices and personnel that support and exercise not only

173

the crippled limb but also the patient's will and hope level, so a caseworker needs for his client the underpinnings of basic economic adequacy and social opportunity. Without these one may, by compassion and the input here and there of some special service or aids, help another to "feel better" and, from this, to "do better." But these small and unreliable gains, that may make effort and endurance possible may not often make change possible or visible. I dare say that our orthopedist friend would protest against any research or judgment that assessed his treatment results if he had nothing more for his patient than bed and board and his tender encouragements.

This is in no sense an argument for social work to abandon the long-and chronically poor or those "multi-problem" families with so many deficits as to be drained of energy or incentive or hope. Such people have long and deep and fully understandable dependency needs. Let us meet them. They may have immutable mental or physical handicaps. Let us protect and provide for them. They may be permeated by hopelessness and apathy or by smolder-ing, volcanic hostility. Let us labor to give them less reason for these. They may, on the basis of some earlier experiences of competence and satisfaction, be waiting for and willing to use the help to find and free their powers once again. Then there is strong potential for their use of help. But to give such help requires not only casework but other programs of social action too. Such other programs have not yet been fully developed or are not yet invented. It requires the implementation of social welfare policies and institutions beyond what we have as yet been able to persuade or mobilize our nation fully to accept—though progress is plain to be seen. It requires that social workers dream the possible dream, and tell it, clearly and re-peatedly and persuasively, and support it with knowledge and know-how. It requires, more, that we recognize that social welfare is not the business and responsibility solely of social work. We may, it is true, need to be the continuous naggers and criers for social justice—the social conscience. But to this righteous indignation and compassionate concern we must add the hard knowledge and the clear perspective that will make us respected partners or informants for the many other professions and organizations for whom some aspects of social welfare are also a central concern.

Is Casework Necessary?

If this is so, then one must face the bottom-layer question, this: Is casework necessary? Since it cannot do all we wish it could, or all we have mistakenly expected it to do, can it be disposed of?

My answer, as a caseworker, is this: "No, casework is not necessary. Yes, it can be disposed of."

It can be disposed of if one is ready to dispose of the idea that there are times and conditions when any one of the mass of human beings may be unable to cope unaided with his problems. It can be disposed of if one believes that any person should be able to use the resources that are available to him and that, if he cannot, that is his hard luck. It is unnecessary if one holds that any person who cannot cope on his own should be left to take the consequences. It can be disposed of if one believes that an individual's aspiration and well-being is of minor concern in our society. It is unnecessary if one believes that all men are in fact created equal and that they do indeed have equal capacities and access to opportunities. It is disposable if one believes that what counts is "humanity," but not individual people.

But if one believes that any person at some time and place and condition may need help over some obstacle to competent and satisfying handling of his work or love tasks; if one believes that people differ one from the other

175

and that, therefore, they may at times need attention attuned to their particular capacities and wishes in their particular situations; if one recognizes that the human dilemma is bled over and wept over not in the faceless mass but by this John and that Mary and this kid; if one believes that the still-lively growth powers and aspirations in one human being may be freed by the caring and guidance of another; if one recognizes, on the basis of historical fact, that the growth of humanness and the development of meaningful self-other relationships rests upon the constant nurture and concern for the individual human being as well as upon a rising floor of basic security—then casework as a process in social work is not dispensable. In short, if we believe in individual worth and are troubled by individual hurt then we must maintain a socially supported mode of helping individuals and families to endure the human condition and more, of influencing them to better it for themselves and for others. Casework is one such mode.

One more "if." If we pose the question, repeatedly raised today, as to whether casework is a process that is or is not successful in helping people lift themselves by their bootstraps, we must first ask and answer the question: "Do the people have boots?"

There is an old story about rigorously trained students in the College of the University of Chicago. It is said that if one asks a plain and simple question of them, such as "Do you love your mother?" the student will answer, "Relative to what?" I have been infected by this rigor, this push for precision and the establishment of basic premises. When I am asked, "Can casework work?" I must answer, "Relative to what? Under what circumstances? To what realistic expectations and ends?" Only when these are validly defined will I be ready to stand up to be judged, whether for whipping or praise.

Casework

and

"The Diminished Man"

I think we are past the peak of the battle against casework. If I am not being made myopic by excesses of weariness or hope, I think we may speak of it in the past tense. It was a battle, waged with lethal accusations and crusader banners whose mottoes spoke to massive need for massive social action programs; in spots there were guerilla attacks, both unexpected and bewildering. At times some of us were bloodied and bowed too; some of us retreated from the turmoil; some of us made our way into the fray in the quest to understand why we were the enemy and what we could or should do to bring about a working coalition with those we considered our professional brothers.

I will admit that I have had my fill of being defender of the faith. It is not that I do not like a good fight about ideas or principles or purposes; I relish that. Being a defender, however, puts one into a heels-dug-into-the-ground position, and I should like to pull out and go exploring forward again. There is much yet to know, to think about and to do, even within the confines of that social work method called casework.

But first, one must take stock. The attackers of

Social Casework, April 1970.

casework had—and have—a point; more than that, they have a just cause. Because of many good and bad reasons that cannot be examined here, the casework method for too many years had come to dominate social work and to be mistakenly equated with it. From nationwide governmental programs to two-person family agencies, there was an implicit belief that if only there were enough well-trained caseworkers, people in trouble could be enabled to cope with their social problems. We had banked on the great government programs of income maintenance and medical care to furnish the foundation for a living. We had lost sight of the forces and powers for human ill-being and misery that remained virulent and widespread, and in the wake of which any individual—client or caseworker—was helpless. As the spokesmen for social work, caseworkers had tacitly promised more than could be delivered by *any* one profession, whatever its nature or modes of operation. Those who attacked it, therefore, were attacking our sometimes naive and unwitting pretenses. They were calling for forms of social action based upon reforms of social policy and programs, some that were within social work's long-marked-out (but scarcely scratched) turf, and some that called for social work alliances with popular and political as well as with other professional sources of power.

It is a long-needed movement that is sweeping through social work now. With some growing sense of their direction and some lessening of their romanticism, the "social actionists"—whether they are community workers, social program planners and developers, consultants and stimulators to grass roots organizations, or government officials—are directing their energies now toward fighting the real enemy. That real enemy is not casework. It is social conditions that pollute social living, not only among the poor—although there the social smog is thickest—but across total communities.

Place and Purpose of Casework

Is there any valid place for casework in the purposes and programs of social work? To answer this question of place and purpose, we must take full cognizance of our identity. Casework is one method in social work. It is not a "thing" that can be "given" to anyone; it is not of itself a service; and it is not an agency program. An agency whose program is to promote family welfare usually *uses* the casework method toward this end. It could commit itself to using a form of group work as its major helping mode, as indeed seems to be the case in those family agencies that are concentrating on family-group treatment. It could conceivably use community work methods, as in the organization of family groups in selected neighborhoods for parent-child socialization purposes. It could effectively use combinations of these three major methods. The casework method has this identifying characteristic: it takes as its unit of attention, as the unit to be helped, one person or one family, suffering some clear and present problem or obstacle to satisfactory or satisfying social functioning, either in carrying necessary tasks or inter-personal relationships.

Is there then a place and purpose in social work for a helping process that, in the midst of recognized widespread social "dis-ease," gives attention to individual men and women and children who are in trouble and who ask for or need help?

If the answer is no, one stands on the edge of nihilism. If one cannot affirm the worth of the individual man one cannot affirm the worth of that man multiplied into mankind. There is no test of a social system or policy except as a measure of its effect upon individual well-being. There is no "love of mankind" except as fraudulent rhetoric, unless there is compassion for a single human being. Casework is based upon the belief in the worth of

179

each single person, whatever his class or creed or color, and upon the concern that when he bleeds he should be attended to. (I am simple-minded enough to say that I am not even averse to "Band-Aids." They are a considerable help in alleviating human hurt and in preventing further complications. They are not substitutes for major surgery nor for the complete reorganization of a hospital system. But this is not their function or their claim. Some services given by the casework method are certainly like Band-Aids. They not only make it possible for persons to carry on their necessary functioning, but they also serve as a preventative measure. Some other services given by the casework method are more closely analogous to more radical forms of medical treatment. In some instances the caseworker must use other forms of social work or other powers for attack upon the social sources of infection or wounds. But the caseworker believes that while these are being found and used, he who suffers must be aided.)

Not only do caseworkers affirm the moral question of each man's worth and right to be given the opportunity to achieve his socially approved goals, but there are some practical considerations too. A person's problems today will not wait for the wheels of justice or social reform to grind out change. Grind they must, and it is hoped that social work will accelerate them. But the man who is their victim wants help *now*, because his problems in personal and family life hurt now. And if these problems are the result of yesterday's causes, they are at the same time the causes of tomorrow's new problems.

We are not so naive as to believe that improved or even "ideal" social opportunities and conditions (whatever those may be) result in human "happiness" (whatever that may be). The evident fact is that improved social conditions bring with them a rising level of expectation within that intransigent, never-satisfied, always striving creature called man. So, while a majority of persons might, under optimal social conditions, find themselves free to use their capacities and opportunities for self and family fulfillment, it is just possible that a substantial minority might find themselves needing or wanting more than they have, and looking to some institutionalized service conveyed in some individualized way.

It is interesting that no other profession has been censured or held culpable because of its individualized help. No one has said to the lawyer, "Shame! You deal with your clients in antiquated courts run by often inadequate personnel and under often archaic law! Stop carrying these cases and attend instead to the necessary reformations in the legal system!" No one has said to the doctors or nurses, "How irresponsible that you waste your time and energies in giving bedside care when there are thousands of people who need but cannot afford medical care, and when, moreover, there remain places in society that daily breed disease and malnutrition and mental sickness!" No one has said to the teachers, "What a waste to give your attention to this child or that who is a maverick in your class, when the whole rotten school system needs overhauling!"

Perhaps the reason lies in what I proposed earlier: that in the past, individual help by the casework method was being proffered *instead* of and not *alongside* other modes of social work. I think—or hope—we are on the border now of mutual agreement: That the casework method is for helping individual people who are the victims (and sometimes the perpetrators) of social or psychological problems. But when the problems beset large sectors of the population, they must be identified, studied, and resolved or mitigated by other methods of social work and other relevant professions and groups.

Finally, I propose that casework serves—or is geared to

serve—one purpose that cannot be brushed aside as trivial. Its existence stubbornly asserts the importance of individual man and of the individual, small, frail clusters of persons called families.

Concept of "The Diminished Man"

We live in an era of "the diminished man."[1] It is not only that the forces of technological and industrial and social organizations by their sweep and magnitude have left man dizzied and dwarfed. It is not only that scientific and technological changes have by their swiftness and potency made him feel increasingly subject to pressures from mechanical and electrical forces that are often not even palpable or visible. It is not only that the boundaries of man's world have shrunk, but that its multiplied population crowds in upon him so that he is threatened with having no place of his own—inside or outside—where he can stand, his feet apart and his arms flailing, to proclaim his necessary territory and his right to be himself.

It is not alone the antihuman forces that have diminished man. He has been diminished and demeaned steadily and grindingly by those very persons we call humanists, those whose métier is man and his works. Of course, humanists also are men. That they suffer the sense of littleness and impotence and loss of purpose in a society that cries havoc as it races ahead to create it is not surprising. But those of us who search their works for some reassuring vision, some sign that man is yet seen as master of some part of his fate, that he is yet "manful" enough to contend with the gods, that he carries in him the spirit to reach beyond his grasp, find instead that he is belittled.

The graphic and plastic arts all but deny his existence:

---

1 This term was used by Archibald MacLeish in "The Revolt of the Diminished Man," *Saturday Review,* 7 (June 1969), p. 16.

sculpture and painting are absorbed in machine forms and movements, or with images of man so atomized, fragmented, and distorted that he is unrecognizable. The theatre depicts him as puny, absurd, and involved in flat, meaningless interplay with other puny, absurd men, or it offers sensation as a substitute for emotion. The novel today presents the nonhero, and deals with men and women who are lost, little, limp; and the author does not mean to rescue them from their limbo. "You are pitful or contemptible," he says of his creatures, "but, too bad, that's the way I see you." (It is interesting how few characters one is able to identify with in the modern novel. With whom have you felt "at one" in a novel of the past five years? When did you last really care about how he or she "came out"?) As for modern music, it takes its themes—if my admittedly reluctant ears hear it rightly—straight from street traffic, the electric waste disposer, the pile driver, and the riveter.

The paradox of it all is that during these past four decades the "cult of personality" has held full sway. Rising both out of Freud's explorations of the inner man and out of the increased environmental ease which made it possible for most of us to turn our eyes from the dangers outside us to those within, the cult of personality affirmed the value, the interesting quality, and even the sacredness of individuality. Indeed, the rapid development of casework in this same period was in large part the result of this consuming new interest. For reasons which cannot be developed here, however, this placing of individual man in the center of our attention resulted not in an enhanced but in a diminished vision of him. He was seen in all his frailty, in all his psychological sicknesses, and in his helplessness.

Perhaps to compensate him for this unfortunate makeup (and for other reasons too), there arose a parallel intensified affirmation of man's right to happiness—not to the *pursuit* of happiness, which is something else again, because pursuit implies a seeking, a quest, or an *effort* to achieve a goal, but to the right to *be* happy, as if this were some stable state, impervious to changes of circumstance or standards. Incidentally, Freud never promised "happiness" as a consequence of self-knowledge and self-management. It was he, I believe, who said that psychoanalysis could help people to overcome the suffering of neurosis in order for them to deal with the suffering in their present-day lives.

But the juxtaposition of an illusory goal that could never be firmly achieved—certainly not by any thinking man—and of human creatures who were increasingly aware of their guilts and mistakes and hostilities and hurts accumulated through no fault of their own, deepened man's pessimism and self-contempt and heightened his sense of being more the victim of his society than an actor in and upon it. Thus we have the paradox of the diminished man. The cult of personality has brought in its wake the demeaning sense of personal ambiguity and helplessness combined with an outraged sense of having been cheated by "society" of a paradise promised but never delivered.

One might have anticipated—perhaps "hoped" is the truer word—that the study of personality would have brought forward some of the wonders in man: the marvels of his foliated, convoluted brain, the untapped founts of his courage and spirit, the remarkable evolutions in his physical makeup that are manifest within even one generation. Each year, somehow, men are able to exceed the running, jumping, swimming records of earlier years; ballet dancers increasingly defy the apparent limits of the body's muscle and bone; children walk and talk earlier, grow taller, get higher Scholastic Aptitude Test scores. These are wonders on which to ponder.

When men stepped on the moon not long ago, there were mixed feelings among many of us that again we had scored a technological miracle, but not one that was humanly significant. Yet one could not overlook the underlying miracle: that all this visible machinery and all these unseen and unseeable formulas and laws by which these men were controlled were the products of men's minds. They had been discovered and brought into use through the activity of the spongy, grey cells inside the small, round head of that "poor, bare forkt animal" called man. The wonders of man's mind have scarcely begun to be fathomed. To move from the cosmos to the microcosm in which our daily experience occurs, there is wonder, too, in the bonds of love and loyalty that hold human beings together, in the compassion and empathy that bind one man to another, and in man's striving not only to realize the self but to use the self in the interest of others.

Caseworkers are human beings (despite some opinions to the contrary), and so they are, by and large, creatures of their times. They were part of the personality cult; they utilized the best behavioral theory and concentrated upon the inadequacies and sickness in man. This was understandable certainly, since those who came to them for help were often, in fact, diminished men, sometimes dwarfed by years of emotional starvation, sometimes twisted or made weak and helpless by the slings and arrows of outrageous circumstances and by the lack of means by which to meet them, sometimes suffering because they knew only hate and anger, or only anxiousness and guilt. As a result they felt themselves to be only half men. For a long time caseworkers too strove for their clients' happiness—that is, strove for goals of "cure" or "all fixed up"; and when, in the natural order of things, they found that such goals could scarcely be achieved, they suffered inevitable discouragement and felt that man was a sorry creature indeed. Thereby they were themselves diminished in their own eyes. Yet, because caseworkers are human beings, there remained burning in them that persistent small flame of hope or faith that said, "But he *does* matter, he *is* worthwhile, his individuality *must* be recognized and respected, he *has* untapped potentials, even the least of his kind." "I will," said the caseworker, "hear the voice and see the face and work toward the enhancement of the individual man."

But now (as we used to say when we were children and our hearts were wrung with the anguish of storybook characters in trouble) comes the *good* part. Some students of personality and of individual man were not satisfied with the dark view of man as the product of a family conspiracy or of a society that chiefly repressed and traumatized him. Whether as a reaction against this view, necessary to achieve some balance, or whether out of that indomitable human spirit that repeatedly rises up to say "but," "what if," and "more yet," personality study began to be focused upon other aspects of man's behavior. The questions for study (I am aware of oversimplifying in the interests of time) became not, How is it that this is such a puny creature, so wanting in adequacy and stature? but rather, How is it that this creature survives at all? How is he able to cope? What does he have in him that makes him push and strive for more? Recent studies into the nature of man, his innate potentials, his growth, and the conditions conducive to his sturdy development in childhood and competence in adulthood point to ego strengths and strategies that are only beginning to be identified and understood. These studies suggest greater powers for coping and problem-solving in man than we had suspected, certainly greater than those we had tapped. They reaffirm to some extent that man is capable of learning to use himself in ways that will enhance his interpersonal and instrumental competence, and hence his sense of his worth and purpose and of finding that enhanced self-image and secured identity in the pursuits of his daily life. This is the promise inherent in the most recent theories of ego psychology and in the supporting research that reveal drives toward competence and greater self-realization.[2]

Whether that promise is fulfilled or is valid will depend on how its underlying postulates are translated into action. Social caseworkers are among those who must do that translation. If we can do it, we would not be merely the advocates for the diminished man; we could become the augmenters and enhancers of man's self-respect, self-confidence, and competence.

Toward the Future

If I were a rhetorician I would stop with this high-sounding sentence. I am, however, a conscience-driven social worker, so I cannot allow myself or you the pleasure of closure by peroration. I have a mounting conviction with which I turn to burden you. It is that if we are to justify casework fully, we must go several steps beyond where we have been. We cannot bask in the virtuous effulgence of our faith in man, nor bank on the cheerful view that there is more to man than we had dreamed of, and that somehow this will out. The "beyond" I refer to is in the direction of contributing to the knowledge of man, of everyday man in his everyday family, involved in everyday love and work tasks.

Because casework has carved out and delimited its unit of attention to the individual man or the individual family, we bear special responsibility for illuminating and exploring the characteristics and behaviors and values of these microcosms of everyday life. It is a kind of privilege for caseworkers to be able to focus on a small unit in an otherwise big and bewildering world. That privilege, as all privileges should, carries with it an equal responsibility: that we produce in greater quantity and with greater

---

2 Some propositions about motivating stimuli in adulthood are developed in greater detail in Helen Harris Perlman, *Persona: Social Role and Personality* (Chicago: University of Chicago Press, 1968).

regularity and reliability some significant data and ideas on the commonplaces of living. Common human needs have been identified. Common human ways of coping with and meeting those needs and common ways of searching for meaning and gratification within common living experiences are as yet only vaguely delineated.

If casework is to be accused of faulting, it is that we have not sufficiently examined the human material and the human milieu in which for decades we have been intimately involved. For one thing, we have diminished ourselves and the people we have dealt with by looking anxiously to what some other profession told us was "important" or "true." We have too often underestimated our own capacity to see and to think by borrowing the glasses and adopting the perspectives of others. Once these were the lenses and perspectives of orthodox psychiatry; if a caseload did not hold at least one whopping instance of an unresolved oedipal conflict, it was because the caseworker was a dud. Of late it has been the social scientist whose viewing lenses we earnestly borrow and through which we peer.

Someone says that the poor are more naturally spontaneous than the nonpoor, and so the caseworker notices spontaneity. If he does not, he doubts himself. If he is bold enough to ask where spontaneity (which is held to be "good") stops and impulsiveness (which is held to be "bad") begins, he is likely to ask it only in private. Someone else says that there is a necessary culture of the poor that social workers who are intransigently middle class do not understand and ought not to meddle with. Is it true? Is it true for this ghetto family—or for that one? Have caseworkers known lower-class families that hoped and aspired to *stay* lower class, that wanted nothing better for themselves than what they had, or were content to wait until the whole opportunity system was overhauled? And if what most lower-class families want is *up* and *out*, would a caseworker not be perpetuating a mockery if he conveyed the idea that only circumstances had to change, not individuals' ways of acting and relating? Where individual destiny is heavily determined by a middle-class educational and industrial system, should the demands of these systems upon individuals be ignored?

Too often overinfluenced by other perceptions and conclusions, the caseworker tends to undervalue what his own eyes and ears tell him. In part he believes the findings of the social scientist because the latter presents generalizations based on quantifications of data gathered in the cool climate of research. We need not and must not underestimate the necessity for and the values to be derived from these contributions from the behavioral sciences. My plea is only that we should not use these findings to *substitute* for, or to obliterate, the special knowledge that the caseworker can provide. That special knowledge is the product of observing people in action—often white-hot, on-the-spot, emotionally charged action—that reveals the very special features of a person who otherwise remains undifferentiated from his class, his ethnic group, or the anonymous mass. If I may resort to some overused but telling phrases, caseworkers are "where the action is" for individual persons as they live out their daily lives, and therefore they can "tell it like it is."

This is admittedly not an easy thing to do. It is not easy to be both an actor and an observer, both a helper and an inquirer. The caseworker is always in the position of being a dynamic part of a transaction. However, if we are to make a contribution to the knowledge of man as a coper and grappler and striver, then we must ourselves grapple with this problem of how to be "participant-observers" in "action research."

Yet another perspective deserves our notice because it too has tended to distort what and how we see. It is our belief in the predominance of evil in man's makeup and condition. Perhaps this belief is valid; maybe there *is* more badness than goodness in each of us and in the world around us. But the subject deserves to be raised as a question to be studied rather than to be taken for granted. We assume that people's anxieties and hostilities, their fears and violences lurk within them waiting for some trauma or license to release them from their tissue-thin bonds. We rarely assume that goodness lies dormant, waiting for some cue to call it forth. Courage, loyalty, social responsibility, social intelligence, compassion— perhaps these too may grow, given the proper stimuli and reinforcement. It is certain that in this scientific age of ours man has been most studied in relation to what has gone awry with him. In the clinic, on the couch, in the caseworker's office, the questions asked are chiefly, How is it that you came to this sorry state? What hurtful experiences have occurred? What hurting actions have you taken that result in this trouble and problem? Only occasionally are questions asked that reveal what a person has experienced or done as good and rewarding; what competences he has known in himself; and what beneficial relationships he has had with other people.

I have often played with the idea of doing some "in-depth" interviewing of people who, by their own testimony and that of the people who best know them, are reasonably content (within the world of their personal lives, that is) and reasonably competent in the performance of the roles they value. I would ask, "Tell me, how did you achieve this? How do you account for your sense of well-being? Surely you must have had disappointments, hurts, frustrations, even trauma in your past life. How did you come out so well? And what do you do now? How do you manage the natural anxieties and crises and frustrations that every human life holds?" Or I would like to confront people at peak points of their lives, when they are graduating from school, or getting married, or being promoted on the job, and ask, "What part did you, as a person with conscious intention and direction, have in making this happen?"

My hunch would be that the persons I accosted would have a hard time answering these questions. Even the most introspective among us would. We are all creatures of our culture, and it has encouraged us to pick and rummage among the tender, hurting spots of our personalities and of our past and present experiences. We have not been taught to examine ourselves and our experiences in relation to our healthy drives or with regard to the complex ways by which we, as individuals and as families, maneuver successfully to achieve our single or common goals. We have not been taught to appreciate and examine our potential or actual capacities. When the questions and inquiries of those who would help us are always, What hurts and what sore spots need examinations? then those inevitably become our central areas of introspection.

Two Suggestions

In brief, I submit two suggestions for caseworkers' new directions. One is that we examine and test the possibility of our being not only participant-helpers but observers and collators of the special phenomena it is our privilege (and responsibility) to observe. The other is that we chart some of the insufficiently explored territory in man's living toward his enhanced sense of self and self-worth.

I confess that I am more sure about *what* we ought to study than *how* to do it. Probably not all caseworkers could be action researchers, and probably not any could be such all the time in all their cases. Perhaps under the aegis of a group of agencies, or of a national body such as the Family Service Association of America, a special study project could be planned, focused upon certain groupings of cases at different times. The caseworkers would need to be selected for their perception and their freedom to question current theory as well as for their ability to question and observe clients. I think most clients would not be averse to taking part in such study. Most people find it interesting and even self-instructive to be asked to explore and explain their feelings and behavior in the pursuit of some common understanding. Everyone, unless he is under crucial stress, likes to be a source of knowledge. There even tends to be a therapeutic reaction on the part of the person whose experiences and ideas have been sought out and respectfully considered; he feels himself to have been a contributor in a quest to understand all human beings. I feel certain, therefore, that we would not need to fear the effect of concentrated study upon persons whose prime involvement would be seeking and getting help.

As for the content of our study, it needs to be a more precise and detailed accounting of man's "inner space." The inner space I refer to is of two sorts: one is within the individual man, contained inside his skin, yet revealing itself always by his words and actions, and penetrated always by the words and actions of other people and circumstances; the second is the inner space of family life—the emotional climate that is contained within the walls of a room or a household, constantly in play among, upon, and within its members.

We know a great deal about the individual. But we know him chiefly as a diminished man. We know families too. We know the strains and stresses and tearing conflicts of unhappy marriages, unhappy parent-child relationships, and something of their cause-effect relationships. But there remain great areas of inner space that wait our further exploration. They consist of the aspects of human personality and interpersonal relationships that spring from the quest for love, from the drive for social attachment, from hope, and the reach for greater self-fulfillment. Of course, these same drives may result in distorted and destroying forms of behavior, but they often result in psychological "haleness" and socially constructive consequences. Under what conditions? What makes them work out well, rather than badly? What do we know of why people are loyal or loving? What do we understand of how family members resolve their inevitable problems of "me" versus "us," "my" versus "ours," "I want" versus "I renounce"?

We need to examine minutely what there is in man's daily life that could become more satisfying, more interesting, and more valued by him. We need to get under surfaces, to plumb in depth the everyday roles that everyday man puts himself into body and soul. What do the roles hold that feeds into his love needs and that meets (or can be molded to meet) his need for social affirmation? What opportunities ought to be provided (or invented) by which man can feel himself more fulfilled? What is the nature of what we call ego strength? What are the behaviors, for instance, that are "coping strategies," as different from "defensive" ones? By what ways can a person's potentials for problem-solving be released? In what diverse ways do people get satisfaction, feel "good," feel themselves to be adequate at least, or effective at best? What makes a man say to himself, "I've had a pretty good day" or "I've got a pretty nice family"?

These are mixed and unordered questions I spill out here. They have a common quest, however. It is the search for what constitutes "health" or "adequacy" or social effectiveness combined with personal gratification within the daily life of man and his family.

Conclusion

Social provisions, essential as they are, generous and utopian though they may be, will not by their presence alone yield a sense of self-as-becoming, of inner fulfill-

193

ment, or of individual stature. These attributes of enhanced "being" arise from a person's consciousness of
himself as a doer, a maker, a user of resources both within
himself and outside, as one who can and does exercise
choice and whose doing and choosing for the most part
yield desired and desirable consequences. These attributes
expand further as a person has some realistic and sensitive
understanding of—and as he pursues—what everyday life
can be expected to hold of satisfaction and reward.

This I propose as our perspective in casework: that man
is not only worth our belief and faith in him, that he is not
only worth our best help when he is troubled, but that he
is worth our curious and wondering study of the nature of
his adaptability, aspirations, and experiences and opportunities that can enrich his daily life. With the accumula-
tion of this further knowledge, we may be able to propose
more surely what men need by way of social provisions
beyond the fill-in of deficits. We may make a much-needed
addition to the understanding of man as a problem-solving
animal, different from every other species by the fact that
he continuously measures what *is* by his conception of
what *ought* to be. Even if it yields less than we hope, in at
least one small corner of the modern world—that life-space
of the social agency that focuses on individuals and
families—there would be in process the effort to enhance
rather than diminish man's image of himself.

I am reminded that on the empty spaces of the moon the
astronauts, guided by scientists, bent down and laboriously
picked up piece by piece of pebble, rock, and stone.
"What's in them?" they asked. "When we examine their
fine particles what might we understand further about the
nature of the universe?" No one thought that was trivial or
useless.

Bibliography of Publications
of Helen Harris Perlman

BOOKS

1. *Social Casework: A Problem-Solving Process.* Chicago: University of Chicago Press, 1957. Translations in Dutch, Swedish, Spanish, Italian, Greek, German, Japanese, and several Asiatic and African languages.
2. *So You Want to Be a Social Worker.* New York: Harper & Row, 1962. Rev. ed., 1970.
3. *Persona: Social Role and Personality.* Chicago: University of Chicago Press, 1968. (French translation in process)
4. *Helping: Charlotte Towle on Social Work and Social Casework.* Edited. Chicago: University of Chicago Press, 1969.

ARTICLES

5. "Casework and the Problem of Jewish Youth," *Jewish Social Service Quarterly* (September 1936).
6. "Professional Development on the Job," *The Family* 19 (April 1938): 42—45.
7. "Content in Basic Social Casework," *Social Service Review* 21 (March 1947): 76—84.
8. "Casework Services in Public Welfare," *Proceedings of the National Conference of Social Work.* New York: Columbia University Press, 1947.
9. "Parable of the Workers of the Field," *Social Service Review* 23 (March 1949): 21—24.
10. "Classroom Teaching of Psychiatric Social Work," *American Journal of Orthopsychiatry* 19 (April 1949): 306—16.
11. "Mental Health Planning for Children," *Child Welfare* 28 (June 1949): 8—9, 16—18.
12. "Generic Aspects of Specific Settings," *Social Service Review* 23 (September 1949): 293—301. Also, *Proceedings of the National Conference of Social Work in the Current Scene.* New York: Columbia University Press, 1950.

Book reviews and nonprofessional writings omitted.

13. "Teaching Casework by the Discussion Method," *Social Service Review* 24 (September 1950): 334–46. Reprinted in *Education for Social Work*. Edited by Eileen Younghusband. London: George Allen & Unwin, Ltd., 1968.

14. "The Lecture as a Method in Teaching Casework," *Social Service Review* 25 (March 1951): 19–32. Reprinted in *Education for Social Work*. Edited by Eileen Younghusband. London: George Allen & Unwin, Ltd., 1968.

15. "Are We Creating Dependency?" *Minnesota Public Welfare* 6 (June 1951). Reprinted in more than fifteen state welfare journals, and in *Social Service Review* 34 (September 1960): 323–33.

16. "The Caseworker's Use of Collateral Information," *Social Casework* 32 (October 1951): 325–33; *Social Welfare Forum*, 1951.

17. "Putting the 'Social' Back in Social Casework," *Child Welfare* 31 (July 1952): 8–9, 14.

18. "Social Components of Casework Practice," *Social Welfare Forum*, National Conference of Social Work, New York: Columbia University Press, 1953.

19. "The Basic Structure of the Casework Process," *Social Service Review* 27 (September 1953): 308–15.

20. Essay Review of *The Nature of Choice in the Casework Process*, by Anita Faatz, *Social Service Review* 27 (December 1953): 431–33.

21. "Of Records and Supervision," *Social Service Review* 28 (March 1954): 83–85.

22. "The Casework Seminar in the Advanced Curriculum," *Social Work Education in the Post-Master's Program*, No. 2. Council on Social Work Education, New York, 1954.

23. "Ballad for Old Age Assistance, 1954," (verse), *Social Service Review* 28 (March 1954): 90.

24. "Brainwashing—A Social Phenomenon of Our Time," *Human Organization* 14 (Fall 1955): 2. The Society for Applied Anthropology, New York, 1955.

25. "Social Casework Counseling," *Psychotherapy and Counseling. Annals of the New York Academy of Sciences.* Vol. 63. Edited by Roy Waldo Miner. The Academy, New York, 1955.

26. "The Client's Treatability," *Social Work* 1 (October 1956): 32–40.

27. "Freud's Contribution to Social Welfare," *Social Service Review* 31 (June 1957): 192–202.

28. "Family Diagnosis: Some Problems," *Social Welfare Forum* and *Casework Papers*, 1958. National Conference on Social Work, New York: Columbia University Press, 1958.

29. "Where Can They Go for Guidance?" *Guiding Children as They Grow*. Edited by Eva H. Grant, National Congress of Parents and Teachers, 1959.

30. "Social Casework Today," *Public Welfare* 17 (April 1959): 51–54, 88–89.

31. "Intake and Some Role Considerations," *Social Casework* 41 (April 1960): 171–77. Reprinted in *Social Casework in the Fifties*. Edited by Cora Kasius. Family Service Association of America, New York, 1962. Also expanded and revised in *Persona: Social Role and Personality*. Chicago: University of Chicago Press, 1968.

32. "Family Diagnosis in Cases of Illness and Disability," *Social Work Practice in Medical Care and Rehabilitation*. Monograph VI. National Association of Social Workers, New York, 1961.

33. "The Role Concept and Social Casework: Some Explorations," *Social Service Review* 35 (December 1961): 370–81. Reprinted in *New Developments in Casework*. Edited by Eileen Younghusband, London: George Allen & Unwin, Ltd., 1965.

34. "The Role Concept and Social Casework: What Is Social Diagnosis?" *Social Service Review* 36 (March 1962): 17–31.

35. "Some Notes on the Waiting List," *Social Casework* 44 (April 1963): 200–205. Reprinted in *Crisis Intervention*. Edited by Howard Parad. Family Service Association of America, New York, 1965.

36. "Unmarried Mothers, Immorality and the A. D. C.," (mimeographed), Florence Crittenton Association of Chicago, Chicago, July 1963.

37. "Identity Problems, Role, and Casework Treatment," *Social Work Practice*, 1963. National Conference on Social Work, Columbia University Press. Also, *Social Service Review* 37 (September 1963): 307–18. Reprinted in *New Developments in Casework*. Edited by Eileen Younghusband. London: George Allen & Unwin, Ltd., 1965, and (revised) in *Persona: Social Role and Personality*. Chicago: University of Chicago Press, 1968.

38. "Unmarried Mothers," *Social Work and Social Problems.* Edited by Nathan Cohen. National Association of Social Workers, York, 1964.

39. "The Charge to the Casework Sequence," *Social Work* 9 (July 1964): 47–55.

40. "Help to Parents of Retarded Children," Canadian Association for Retarded Children, Toronto, Ontario, October 1964. Reprinted in *Social Work and Mental Retardation.* Edited by Meyer Schreiber. New York: John Day & Co., 1970.

41. "Teaching Social Policy," *International Journal of Social Work* 8 (January 1965): 22–25.

42. "Social Work Method: A Review of the Past Decade," *Social Work* 10 (October 1965): 166–79. Reprinted in *Social Work Practice and Knowledge.* National Association of Social Workers, New York, 1966.

43. "Self-Determination: Reality or Illusion?" *Social Service Review* 39 (December 1965): 410–21. Reprinted in *Values in Social Work,* Monograph IX, National Association of Social Workers, New York, 1967.

44. "An Approach to Social Work Problems: Perspectives on the Unmarried Mother on A. D. C.," *Program Development for Social Services in Public Assistance.* U. S. Department of Health, Education, and Welfare, Bureau of Family Services, Washington, D. C., 1965.

45. "Social Diagnosis Leading to Social Treatment," *Social Work in Child Health Projects for Mentally Retarded Children.* Department of Public Health, Government Printing Office, Washington, D. C., 1965.

46. "Preface" to *Common Human Needs,* by Charlotte Towle (revised edition). National Association of Social Workers, 1965.

47. "Social Casework," *Encyclopedia of Social Work,* 1965. National Association of Social Workers, New York.

48. "Casework Is Dead," *Social Casework* 48 (January 1967): 22–25.

49. "A Note on Sibling," *American Journal of Othropsychiatry* 37 (January 1967): 148–49.

50. "—and Gladly Teach," *Journal of Education for Social Work* 3 (Spring 1967): 41–50. Reprinted in *The Social Work Educator.* Edited by Joseph Soffen. Council on Social Work

Education, 1969; and (abridged) as "Great Teachers," *University of Chicago Magazine* (November-December 1968).

51. "Observations on Services and Research," *Unmarried Parenthood*. National Council on Illegitimacy, New York, 1967.

52. "The Neighborhood Sub-professional Worker—Comments," *Children* 15 (January-February 1968): 12—13.

53. "Casework and the Case of Chemung County," in *The Multi-Problem Dilemma*. Edited by Gordon E. Brown. Metuchen, New Jersey: Scarecrow Press, 1968.

54. "Can Casework Work?" *Social Service Review* 42 (December 1968): 435—37.

55. "Preface" to *Brief and Extended Casework*, by William Reid and Anne Shyne. New York: Columbia University Press, 1969.

56. "Crisis and the Unmarried Mother," *The New Face of Social Work*. Proceedings Spence-Chapin Adoption Service, 25th Anniversary, New York, 1969.

57. Essay Review of *Differential Diagnosis and Treatment in Social Work*, by Francis Turner, "Diagnosis, Anyone?" *Psychiatry and Social Science Review* 3 (August 1969).

58. "Casework and 'The Diminished Man,'" *Social Casework* 51 (April 1970): 216—24.

59. "The Problem-Solving Model in Casework," in *Theories of Social Casework*. Edited by Robert W. Roberts and Robert Nee. Chicago: University of Chicago Press, 1970.

60. "The Problem-Solving Model in Casework," *Encyclopedia of Social Work*, 1971. National Association of Social Workers, New York.

61. "Women in a University." An address (mimeo) to the Trustees and Faculty of the University of Chicago. Reprinted (condensed) in *School Review* 79:1 (November 1970), and in Education Digest (February 1971) as "The Case Against Unisex."